IMAGES
of America

DETROIT
YACHT CLUB

T0274663

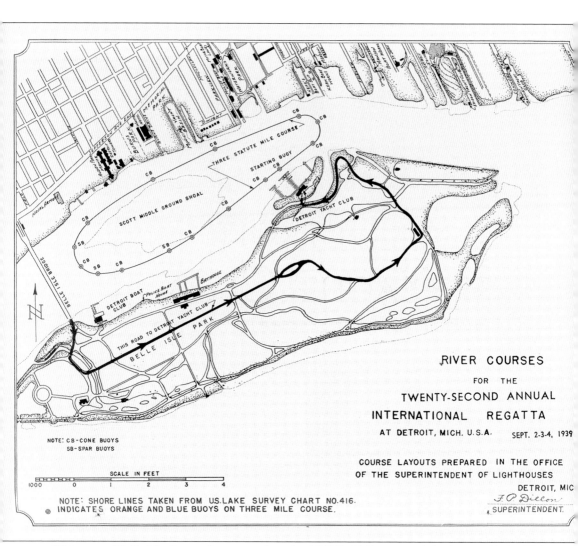

RIVER COURSES

FOR THE

TWENTY-SECOND ANNUAL

INTERNATIONAL REGATTA

AT DETROIT, MICH. U.S.A.   SEPT. 2-3-4, 1939

COURSE LAYOUTS PREPARED IN THE OFFICE
OF THE SUPERINTENDENT OF LIGHTHOUSES

DETROIT, MIC

F. P. Dillon

SUPERINTENDENT.

NOTE: CB-CONE BUOYS
SB-SPAR BUOYS

SCALE IN FEET

NOTE: SHORE LINES TAKEN FROM US.LAKE SURVEY CHART NO.416.
INDICATES ORANGE AND BLUE BUOYS ON THREE MILE COURSE.

This map of Belle Isle directs those attending the 1939 Gold Cup toward the Detroit Yacht Club (DYC). The three-mile racecourse can be seen between the Detroit shore and Belle Isle on the Detroit River. The DYC's small island, with its three docks, is visible at the northern end of Belle Isle. (Courtesy of the Detroit Yacht Club.)

ON THE COVER: The sailboat in the foreground leaves the Detroit Yacht Club harbor on August 26, 1941. The boat is dressed up for the fleet review, the opening ceremony of Venetian Night, when the DYC fleet parades past the commodore's flagship followed by cocktail parties aboard yachts and dinner in the clubhouse, then music, dancing, and entertainment. (Courtesy of the Library of Congress, Prints & Photographs Division.)

IMAGES
of America

DETROIT
YACHT CLUB

John Gibson and Toni Michnovicz Gibson

ARCADIA
PUBLISHING

Published by Arcadia Publishing
Charleston, South Carolina

Printed in the United States of America

Library of Congress Control Number: 2022934562

For all general information, please contact Arcadia Publishing:
Telephone 843-853-2070
Fax 843-853-0044
E-mail sales@arcadiapublishing.com
For customer service and orders:
Toll-Free 1-888-313-2665

Visit us on the Internet at www.arcadiapublishing.com

For our grandchildren—
Julia, J.P., Luke, Wesley, Daphne, Dax, and Dove.

CONTENTS

ACKNOWLEDGMENTS

Among those who deserve thanks are the individual private collections of Detroit Yacht Club members named and the staff of the following archives and libraries. The images in this volume appear courtesy of the Archives of Michigan (AOM); Associated Press (AP); Barlow family collection (BFC); Center for Archival Collections, Bowling Green State University (BGSU-CAC); Historical Collections of the Great Lakes, Bowling Green State University (BGSU-HC); Burton Historical Collection, Detroit Public Library (BHC); Detroit Historical Society (DHS) Detroit Yacht Club Collection (DYCC); Detroit Yacht Club Collection, photography by Mary Schroeder (DYCC-MS); Detroit Yacht Club Collection, photography by Charlie Nick (DYCC-CN); Detroit Yacht Club Foundation (DYCF); Ernie Harwell Sports Collection, Detroit Public Library (EHSC); Edwin Theisen collection (ETC); Estate of F. Peirce Williams (FPW); Gmeiner family collection (GFC); Heller family collection (HFC); History Miami Museum (HMM); Howard Riley collection (HRC); Library of Congress, Prints & Photographs Division (LOC); Martin Chumiecki collection (MCC); Mark Weber collection (MWC); Michael Alberts collection (MAC); Minnesota Historical Society (MNHS); Olds Family Archives—Stephens family (OFA-SF); Patricia Thull-O'Brien collection (PTOC); National Automotive History Collection, Detroit Public Library (NAHC); Collections of The Henry Ford (THF); and the Walter P. Reuther Library, Archives of Labor and Urban Affairs, Wayne State University (WSU).

We also wish to extend our thanks to all those who gave of their time to read the draft and suggest improvements: Bill Lynch, Mark Lifter, Gordon Didier, and Elaine Didier. None of these individuals is responsible for any errors that may have crept into this book.

INTRODUCTION

The Detroit Yacht Club has been a part of the fabric of the city of Detroit and southeast Michigan for more than 150 years. The historical marker that graces the front of the yacht club reads, "Established 1868." According to tradition, the club was founded in 1868 when six men met in the office of a lawyer in downtown Detroit to form a syndicate, purchase a sailboat, and race competitively. Wayne County records show articles of incorporation for the DYC in 1887 and 1895.

The September 22, 1868, edition of the *Detroit Free Press* featured a front-page article that read, "Yacht Regatta . . . We understand that a number of the fine sailing yachts owned in this city and locality, have determined to enter into a friendly contest of sailing qualities. It is expected that the following yachts will take part in the race. The *Coral*, commanded by K. C. Barker; *Humming Bird*, Joseph Nicholson; *Collins*, H. Hackett; *Norma*, J. Lorimer; *Ripple*, Geo. Field." In the "City of the Straits" as Detroit was known, yachting was newsworthy.

Joseph Nicholson was one of those who took part in that "friendly contest of sailing qualities" in 1868. He also competed the next year and won the rematch, and his name continued to surface in the world of boating. Along with winning races aboard the *Hummingbird*, Nicholson achieved success in the marine industry. He made news as captain of the steamship *Planet*, which served the ports of Cleveland, Detroit, and Lake Superior in 1856, and later worked as an inspector of vessels for Lloyd's Marine Insurance Association. He was even noted for doubling the size of his house at 408 Lafayette Avenue at an estimated cost of $10,000.

Another well-known yachtsman at that time was Stephen Ives. He raced the *Ida* and the *Surprise* and won 22 championship flags. It was at his store on Woodward Avenue that an organizational meeting was held on May 31, 1878. The *Detroit Free Press* reported, "the Detroit Yacht Club was organized and named officers . . . with Stephen Ives the treasurer." A regatta followed later that summer. Nicholson was on the DYC regatta committee and Ives raced his yacht *Ida*, finishing in second place. News of the affair was positive: "Yachting matters have been at a standstill in this city," wrote the *Free Press*, "and nothing worthy to be called a yacht club has existed until about two months ago when the Detroit Yacht Club was organized . . . and the first regatta . . . most successfully brought to a close."

Newspaper accounts make it clear that Nicholson and Ives were founding members of the club. Both men's obituaries paint pictures of marine achievement. The headline for Ives's obituary stated he was a "Well-Known Yachtsman." Nicholson's obituary noted his membership in local yacht clubs and said he was "a most efficient major domo in all events of a public character where marine conveniences were available." Nicholson was on the DYC board of directors when the club's 1895 incorporation papers were filed with the county clerk. That application for incorporation included a statement that the DYC began in 1868. Nicholson certainly would have known this to be true, as he was sailing aboard the *Hummingbird* in that year.

The years when Ives and Nicholson were making the news were the days of the Detroit Yacht Club, the Detroit Boat Club, the Citizens' Yachting Association, the West End Yacht Club, and the Michigan Yacht Club. These clubs were spread up and down the Detroit River alongside farms and commercial docks. As the river became increasingly industrialized, clubs chose new locations.

One of these was Belle Isle. The island in the Detroit River was already a popular spot for picnics when the City of Detroit purchased it from the Campau family in 1879. The Michigan Yacht Club moved to Belle Isle in 1892, but ended its stay three years later when overspending forced it into bankruptcy. The DYC purchased the Michigan Yacht Club's clubhouse and has been on Belle Isle ever since.

The Detroit Yacht Club's growth took a dramatic step forward in the early 1920s under the leadership of Commodores Gus Schantz and Gar Wood, who set in motion plans to build the current clubhouse. The membership approved their plans to finance the construction with the sale of bonds. For six of the seven years from 1918 through 1924, either Schantz or Wood served as commodore while the DYC underwent a major transformation. In January 1922, the club had 2,200 members. The grand opening of the new clubhouse on Memorial Day 1923 propelled the club to the center of Detroit society. By 1927, the club's membership had risen to 3,226. It was the largest clubhouse in the United States.

At the same time, the United States experienced dramatic changes in technology. In 1908, Henry Ford's Model T put America on wheels. Detroit's first radio station, WWJ, started broadcasting in 1920. And Gus Schantz welcomed the first flying boat to land in the DYC harbor in 1921. Power boats replaced sailboats in popularity. Speed boat racing ascended, and Detroit became its center.

The fortunes of the Detroit Yacht Club have often reflected those of the city of Detroit. When the current clubhouse was built, Detroit was the automotive capital of the world. Members of the Ford, Fisher, Dodge, Joy, Metzger, and Olds families all belonged to the DYC. The 1929 stock market crash had an impact as well. To cut costs, the board of directors boarded over the indoor pool, which temporarily served as a gym for ping pong, volleyball, and badminton. But the club never defaulted on its bonds.

The changes in American society made it clear that in order to survive and prosper, the Detroit Yacht Club had to adapt. In 1961, the club magazine *Mainsheet* stated, "the DYC was founded as a club for men. There will probably never be a lady commodore." However, wiser heads prevailed. Since 1982, women have served on the board of directors. The new millennium ushered in another long anticipated change with the election of female and African American commodores.

Detroit has seen good times and hard times, riots, and a major decrease in population driven by the dramatic growth of the suburbs. The city hit bottom with a bankruptcy filing in 2013. But Detroit's fortunes and those of the DYC have been improving ever since. The club's membership is more than 800 and growing. Its finances are stable, and the harbor is full of members' boats. All of this bodes well for the future of the Detroit Yacht Club in the decades to come.

One

CLUBHOUSES

When the Detroit Yacht Club celebrated its grand opening on May 30, 1923, almost 5,000 people came for a tour of the biggest yacht club in the world. At the dedication, Sen. James Couzens was the guest speaker, and Commodore Gar Wood received the key to the building. The dining, dancing, and celebrations continued into the night. Later that week, the DYC invited the Detroit Boat Club and the Detroit Athletic Club to private receptions. The DYC was proud to show everyone its handsome building.

That celebratory year for the new Belle Isle clubhouse was in 1923, but the history of the DYC clubhouses begins much earlier. This was the newest clubhouse, but it was not the first. In fact, it was the club's fifth. The first was a building leased from the Centennial Boating and Athletic Association adjacent to Parke, Davis & Company, a Detroit pharmaceutical firm. The club also leased anchorage from the company.

A shuffling of boating clubs began in the late 1880s. The Detroit River was becoming more industrialized and busy with heavy traffic, and clubs were looking for more space. In 1885, the Michigan Yacht Club moved to the edge of the Detroit city limits across from Belle Isle. That was followed by its second move onto Belle Isle, which would be a key to the future of the Detroit Yacht Club.

But the DYC was still downstream. It bought a Detroit Railway Company building and moved it upstream to the Park House Hotel waterfront. The members sailed from there. Meanwhile, the Michigan Yacht Club enjoyed its splendid location on Belle Isle. But the Michigan Yacht Club made some unwise expenditures, and its finances deteriorated. It declared bankruptcy in 1895.

That is when the DYC bought the Michigan Yacht Club building and gained a home on Belle Isle. Though that structure was lost in a 1904 fire, the DYC rebuilt immediately. The club continued to grow. And in the club's next daring and imaginative move, George Mason was hired to work on a grand palace of 93,000 square feet. And what a place it was going to be.

A portion of Stephen Ives's jewelry store at the corner of Woodward Avenue and East Congress Street is just visible at the far-right edge of this photograph. On May 31, 1878, the *Detroit Free Press* reported "a meeting of yachtsmen was held at the office of S. H. Ives last evening, when the Detroit Yacht Club was organized." (BHC.)

In 1886, the Detroit Yacht Club leased Parke, Davis & Company's harbor, which was between Joseph Campau Street and McDougall Street. George Newberry was elected commodore in 1887, and he took advantage of a new law allowing fraternal organizations the right to incorporate, which the DYC did on November 7, 1887. (DHS.)

DYC commodore James Skiffington was a widely respected sailing master. He provided the first ferry service to Belle Isle and was captain of Sen. James McMillan's steam yacht the *Idler*. In 1884, the Detroit Yacht Club lost members to the Michigan Yacht Club and almost collapsed. However, Skiffington, with the help of George Newberry, revived the club in 1886. Skiffington is pictured here with his sons, from left to right, Alfred (reclining), Hubert (arms crossed), Harry, and Truman. (DYCC.)

Upstream from the Parke, Davis & Company harbor was the Centennial Boating and Athletic Association's boathouse. It was at the foot of McDougall Street on the Detroit riverfront. The Detroit Yacht Club membership was increasing, and it could afford a better location. In 1886, the DYC rented this clubhouse and remained there until 1891. (BHC.)

In 1889, the Belle Isle Bridge was built across the American Channel of the Detroit River. It blocked yachtsmen's easy access to Lake St. Clair and forced the Michigan Yacht Club to move because the bridge was built on its property. The Michigan Yacht Club moved to Belle Isle. Meanwhile, the Detroit Yacht Club was still downstream on a busy waterfront that was more polluted and less desirable. (DHS.)

Though there was some reluctance to leave the Centennial Boating and Athletic Association's clubhouse at the foot of McDougall Street, the DYC moved upstream in 1891. The small white building at center, to the left of the ferry dock, was the DYC's second clubhouse. The club bought this building from the Detroit City Railway Company and placed it on the Park House Hotel waterfront across the river from the Michigan Yacht Club on Belle Isle. (BHC.)

The bridge was a problem. It would swing open horizontally, allowing marine traffic to pass, but its schedule was unreliable. DYC commodore Charles Kotcher remembered having to wait up to 30 minutes before the bridge would open. Most members liked the upstream location, but some did not want to start their races from the Park House Hotel's dock. One faction wanted races to start at the McDougal dock, so they left the club and formed the Citizens' Yachting Association and raced downriver from the dock to Twenty-fourth Street and back. The others stayed at the new location. (BHC.)

The move across the river onto Belle Isle was desirable for the Michigan Yacht Club. It now had a premier location and clubhouse. The same Belle Isle Bridge that forced the club to move was now the access it needed to bring members to its new location. And they came by horse and carriage to this new club at the intersection of Inselruhe Avenue and Riverbank Drive. (BHC.)

The Michigan Yacht Club held a huge reception in 1893 for the *Nina*, *Pinta*, and *Santa Maria* when the replica ships were on their way to the World's Columbian Exposition in Chicago. The club still owed $4,200 for its clubhouse, and this reception added $2,275 to the club's debt. Yachtsmen became convinced that social events were the primary focus, rather than sailing, and left the club. The Michigan Yacht Club declared bankruptcy, and the Detroit Yacht Club purchased the building at auction on April 4, 1895. The DYC now had a place on Belle Isle, its third clubhouse. (DYC.)

In 1904, a fire broke out while the steward, his wife, the janitor, and two waitresses were sleeping in the clubhouse. They escaped, but the building burned to the ground. The club received permission from the US secretary of war to build farther out into the water. This clubhouse was designed by Field, Hinchman, and Smith. It had a boat room and locker rooms on the first floor, a 2,000-square-foot ballroom, a ladies' parlor room on the second floor, and a wide veranda around the entire building. The club celebrated with a dance in the ballroom on June 22, 1905. (WSU.)

Pictured here is the Rushmere Fishing and Shooting Club on Harsens Island, which the DYC rented in the summer of 1919. This was a temporary measure while plans were discussed for either enlarging the current DYC clubhouse or building a new one. Gus Schantz suggested purchasing the Rushmere club and bringing it down to Belle Isle piece by piece via barge. In December, the DYC membership decided not to buy the Rushmere club and instead considered an expansion to the current DYC clubhouse. (LC.)

Two years later, the City of Detroit wanted the DYC to leave Belle Isle. However, building a new clubhouse was a priority for Garfield Arthur "Gar" Wood, a Detroit industrialist. He agreed to be nominated for commodore in 1921 if those who encouraged him to run supported his plan to build a new clubhouse. From his winter home in Miami Beach, Gar Wood ran unopposed for commodore, and his entire slate of candidates was elected to the board of directors. Wood's election signaled that the club was ready to build. (LC.)

In 1921, after extensive negotiations, the Detroit Yacht Club agreed to build a new island. In return, the City of Detroit agreed to transfer the DYC's old lease to this new island location, and the DYC would give its old clubhouse to the city. By May 1921, the George D. Mason Company had already let contracts for pile driving, concrete, electrical, and sheet metal work. The first 45-foot test pile was driven by the Candler Dock and Dredge Company on October 5, 1921. (BHC.)

Here is the causeway to the Detroit Yacht Club's new island on April 15, 1922, one week before the cornerstone was laid. The island was created by trucking in dirt from downtown Detroit construction sites; from rocks that came from the widening of the Livingstone channel, a downriver channel west of Bois Blanc Island in the Detroit River; and from hydraulic dredging. (BHC.)

The board of directors led a parade on Belle Isle from the old clubhouse on April 22, 1922, to lay the cornerstone for the new building. The city was glad to let the DYC build a new clubhouse because it wanted to tear down the old clubhouse and increase the island's bathing beach. The city also hoped that the new island would cause the current to run along the shoreline of the bathing beach, thereby keeping the water cleaner. (WSU.)

Commodore Gar Wood set the cornerstone with a silver trowel of mortar. According to the *Detroit Free Press*, a history of the Detroit Yacht Club that was compiled by past commodore Harry Kendall was placed inside the hollow cornerstone. Past commodore Arnold Augustus "Gus" Schantz served as master of ceremonies. The event was marked by speeches from Alex Groesbeck, governor of Michigan; James Couzens, mayor of Detroit; and Edward G. Heckel, commissioner of parks and boulevards. All of these men were members of the club. (WSU.)

The tile and lane markings are yet to come, but the poured concrete provides the outline of the DYC's future indoor pool. Swimming was becoming a popular form of recreation. The club sponsored a swim meet for the city on August 17, 1919, in the Detroit River. Commodore Gus Schantz distributed the prizes after the meet. In 1924, the Detroit Women's City Club constructed its building with a pool, and the Woman's Aquatic Club began its annual one-mile swim from the Edison Boat Club to the Detroit Yacht Club. A pool was a necessity for the new clubhouse. (BHC.)

On July 15, 1922, three months after the cornerstone ceremony, significant progress had been made on the 93,658-square-foot clubhouse. During construction, Gus Schantz, chairman of the building committee, spent hours with the builders and architects. The original George D. Mason & Company contracts that were issued in May 1921 called for building a two-story clubhouse. By January 1922, the plans had been altered, and the A. Albrecht Company was contracted to construct a $500,000, three-story building. (BHC.)

In summer 1929, Gus Schantz, president of the Detroit and Cleveland Navigation Company, began a flying boat service between Detroit, Cleveland, and Buffalo. When he was not running the largest passenger and package freight boat line on freshwater, he chaired the DYC building committee. During construction, only $400,000 in bonds had been sold. Another $100,000 was needed at once, or the work would be stopped. To secure a loan, Schantz offered the Union Guardian Trust Company the remaining $100,000 in unsold DYC bonds as collateral. The company turned him down unless he personally guaranteed the loan in writing. This was the bankers' polite way of telling Schantz no. To their surprise, Schantz agreed to personally guarantee the loan, which was the equivalent of over $1.25 million today. The money was secured, and construction continued. Originally, the new clubhouse was expected to cost $500,000, paid for by selling 20-year bonds paying six-percent interest. The actual cost, including two docks and site preparation, was $708,685.55. At the grand opening of the clubhouse on May 30, 1923, there were thousands of dollars in bonds yet to be sold. As an incentive to join sooner rather than later, the initiation fee was raised $50 with every group of 200 new members who joined. (WSU.)

The club library was just off the second-floor lobby. Here, multiple copies of the daily Detroit newspapers are arranged on the table for members to read. The exterior door was removed when an elevator was added to the building in 1960. (ETC.)

The DYC's new clubhouse included a nursery room, pictured here. At the grand opening, the *Detroit Free Press* described the Detroit Yacht Club as "essentially a man's club" but with "conveniences dear to the heart of a woman." Those features thought appealing to women were a women's locker room with maid service, appliances for quickly drying swimming suits, a powder room, and the provision of childcare in the clubhouse nursery room. The dividing wall on the right has since been removed, and the space is now called the Silver Cup Room. (ETC.)

Here is the billiard room as it appeared in 1923 when the clubhouse was finished. The pool tables were removed in 1941 and the lighting fixtures changed, and it became a card room. For many years, on Friday nights during the winter, men played duplicate bridge starting at 8:30, followed by food and prizes. This is now the Sweepstakes Room and hosts award presentations, receptions, and the annual Sweepstakes cocktail party. (ETC.)

Fred G.W. Cooper, dining room manager, inspects the chef's latest creation in the kitchen. The clubhouse opened in 1923 with six dining areas, which included the main dining room, coffee shop, dining terrace, refreshment veranda, Sailor's Grill (for men only), and a private dining room. The Sailor's Grill became the Grill Dining Room, and the refreshment veranda facing the lagoon was enclosed in 1924 to enlarge the kitchen. The private dining room is now the Harmsworth Room. (ETC.)

On the second floor, the coffee shop was at the entrance to the main dining room. The doors on the right led to the dining terrace, which was redesigned in 1925 so that it could be completely enclosed in the winter and opened in the summer. In 1949, the dining terrace became the women's River Vista Cocktail Lounge. According to the *Mainsheet*, men were permitted in the cocktail lounge when "escorting a feminine companion," but stags were not allowed. The men had their own bar downstairs. (ETC.)

The ceiling of the main dining room featured starfish, crabs, and lobsters in bas-relief, and according to the *Mainsheet*, was finished in gold leaf and tinted coloring. The room could seat over 300, and in the summer, the six dining rooms could accommodate 800 diners at one sitting. The main dining room, the coffee shop, the River Vista Cocktail Lounge, and the downstairs Grill Dining Room were air-conditioned in 1948. (ETC.)

Now called Peacock Alley, this was originally the ladies' lounge. Some claim the name derives from when potential new members and their wives were interviewed here. Others claim the name is derived from the long hallway in the Waldorf-Astoria hotel in New York City, where society ladies once gathered for tea. The floors seen here were executed by the Martin-Gibson Company, tile contractors for the construction of the clubhouse. According to the *Mainsheet*, they used "stock tile laid in interesting patterns." (DYCC.)

The DYC natatorium is one of the few remaining historic indoor pools in the Detroit area. The pool is 25 feet wide, 75 feet long, ranges from 3 feet to 9.5 feet deep, and holds 8,500 gallons of water. The pool was built at full tournament size, the standard size for competitions until larger Olympic size pools were declared the new standard in 1924. Pewabic tile, with its unique appearance, is visible on the pool deck and the walls. (DYCC.)

The men's lounge, with reading lamps, chairs, and comfortable sofas placed next to the large fireplace, is now the Trophy Room. Today, there are over 150 trophies displayed in custom-built cabinets here. According to the *Mainsheet*, the room was proclaimed "the one room reserved for the members, sans wives, daughters or sweethearts." By 1927, the DYC had a total membership of 3,226, of whom 49 were women. More women joined over the years, but they still were not allowed in the men's lounge until 1971. (DYCC.)

This was a gymnasium until it was redesigned as a lounge in 1927. It was remodeled under the direction of Arthur Keil, an architect and a member of the DYC. As the Trophy Room was originally the men's lounge and Peacock Alley was originally the ladies' lounge, the redesign of this room addressed a need for a general lounge where both men and women could meet. It is now the East Lounge, and a bar was added in 1994. (ETC.)

The largest room in the clubhouse, the grand ballroom, was designed before air-conditioning and with dancing in mind. It combined a very high ceiling, doors on either side, and clerestory windows allowing cross ventilation. The arched glass doors at the far end led to the gymnasium in 1923. It was always understood that the gymnasium could be used as part of the ballroom when a large crowd was present, such as the annual Officers' Ball. (DYCC.)

The main dock extended 470 feet from the shore, and was capped by a 350-foot-long dock parallel to the shoreline. The wells on the main dock varied in size from 15 to 35 feet wide and 35 to 125 feet in length. The smaller dock on the right was eight feet wide and extended 220 feet into the river. The main dock was finished 10 days before the 1923 Gold Cup regatta, which started on August 30. The club's island, measuring 11.68 acres, was barren in the beginning, until landscaping, parking, and outbuildings were added over the years. (WSU.)

Two

SAILBOAT RACING

When the Detroit Yacht Club was founded, sailing was not the main thing. It was the only thing. Detroit became the most prominent yachting city on the Great Lakes. For the first few years, the DYC always focused on planning the next regatta. The grand sailboats of the club, the *Puritana*, the *Surprise*, and the *Thetis*, could each comfortably fit 20. By the end of the 1890s, yachts were evolving, sacrificing size and comfort for one thing: speed.

The *Frances A.*, owned by Alex McLeod, and the *Bounce*, owned by David Buick, were smaller than the grand old boats but faster. Both raced in the first annual DYC Sweepstakes Regatta on Lake St. Clair in 1897. By 1898, catboat racing became popular at the club. The *Detroit Free Press* suggested weekly catboat races for the club and offered a handsome silver trophy to the winner. The races were so attractive that the club grew to 366 members, and its debt was wiped out.

Detroit Yacht Club commodore Harry Kendall and Detroit Boat Club commodore Harry Austin formed an organization in 1912 called the Detroit River Yachting Association. This organization of clubs maintained a regatta calendar and a uniform set of racing rules for the yacht clubs and their sailors, thereby eliminating scheduling conflicts. It is now known as the Detroit Regional Yacht-racing Association.

Commodore Harry Kendall also served on a committee with Commodore Henry Clough of the Port Huron Yacht Club and Commodore W.G. Sheehan of the Bayview Yacht Club; together, they organized the first Port Huron to Mackinac Race in 1925. This event is still held every year and is one of the longest freshwater races in the world. The most famous DYC sailor of that race was Commodore Toot Gmeiner on *Apache*, who won the race in 1942, 1943, 1945, 1959, and 1963.

Members can still learn to sail at the Detroit Yacht Club. James McGuire, former DYC Flying Scot program chairperson, said, "learning to sail here at the DYC could be the best decision you can make."

Stephen Ives, who served as treasurer of the Detroit Yacht Club in 1878, owned the *Surprise*, one of the largest sailboats in the club fleet. The *Surprise*, with Charles Boston as skipper, sailed in over 100 races, collected 22 championship flags, and, according to the *Detroit Free Press*, won the Governor Hazen S. Pingree Punch Bowl and Championship Flag in 1897. Ives owned the jewelry store where the yacht club had its organizational meetings. (BHC.)

A tugboat's smoke billows as it tows sailboats to the starting point of a distant regatta. This was a common sight on the Detroit River in the 1890s. The Detroit Yacht Club's biggest sailing disaster occurred on July 3, 1891, when a tugboat similar to this one was towing 27 DYC sailboats to the Anchor Bay Fourth of July regatta. That night, the tugboat was struck by gale force winds, went two miles off course, and ran hard aground. Few sailboats escaped. Most in the tow line crashed into the tugboat or one another and were badly damaged. (WSU.)

In the summer of 1891, a disagreement erupted when DYC commodore Christian Lichtenberg told the crew of the *Aldina R* that their race victory was nullified and that the *Madeline* had won instead. The *Aldina R* crew was celebrating the victory at the Park House Hotel when they were told. They appealed the commodore's ruling and lost. Two weeks later, many DYC members, including John Ackerman of *Thetis* (right), and the *Aldina R* crew, quit the club and formed the Citizens' Yachting Association with Ackerman as vice commodore. (LC.)

DYC member Matthew Kramer and his crew aboard the *Josephine* heel over as they compete on August 29, 1892. This regatta was hosted by the Citizens' Yachting Association, and the race started at its McDougall dock on the Detroit River. In 1891, when the Detroit Yacht Club split into the DYC and the Citizens' Yachting Association, the competition became keener as the two clubs raced against each other. (BHC.)

The sailboat *Detroit*, pictured here at the Michigan Yacht and Power Company Works, was financed by Detroit Yacht Club members. It was built to compete for the Canada Cup in 1901 but lost in the preliminary trials to the *Cadillac*, which was sponsored by the Detroit Boat Club. The only time the *Detroit* beat the *Cadillac* was when DYC member Alex McLeod was the skipper. Over the next two years with McLeod at the helm, the *Detroit* beat the *Cadillac* a total of four times. The magazine *Sail and Sweep* declared McLeod "one of the cleverest sailors on fresh water." (LC.)

Detroit Yacht Club member Pete Hobart on the *Mermaid* (left) beat the *Cleveland* and the *Toledo* at the annual Inter-Lake Yachting Association's Put-in-Bay Regatta in 1906. In 1885, Alex McLeod, a future DYC commodore, helped organize the Inter-Lake Yachting Association and served as its commodore in 1898. Other DYC commodores who served as commodores of the Inter-Lake Yachting Association were Harry Kendall, 1915; Charles Kotcher, 1922; Otto Barthel, 1924; Gus Schantz, 1926; Mark Hanna, 1929; Gar Wood, 1935; Andrew Hackett, 1939; and Albert Grundy, 1952. (LC.)

Herman Schmidt's *Spray*, a 21 footer, lashed a broomstick to the mast in 1906 to proclaim his clean sweep of the *Cherry Circle* four times that summer. At season's end, Schmidt sold the *Spray* to Fred Price of Chicago's Columbia Yacht Club. Schmidt had already won the Hotel Ste. Claire Cup twice racing *Spray*. If *Spray* won the race a third time, the cup would go to the owner of *Spray*. Therefore, when Schmidt sold the *Spray* to Price, it was agreed that if Price won the Hotel Ste. Claire Cup racing *Spray*, he would give the cup to Schmidt. Price's *Spray* won the race in 1909, and DYC commodore Schmidt had to go to court to secure the cup from Price. Schmidt gave the cup to the Detroit Yacht Club in 1911. (BHC.)

DYC commodore Charles Sieder, a starting cannon between his legs, is pictured with his crew holding the 1910 Universal Class D championship flag awarded by the Inter-Lake Yachting Association. Every year, the association sponsored a week of sailboat and powerboat racing at Put-in-Bay on Lake Erie. The week began with a men's-only party called a smoker, which featured cigars, bourbon, and speeches. The week ended with the commodore's fleet review, the Yachtsman's Ball, and the distribution of trophies and flags. (HRC.)

DYC commodore Charles Sieder and crew are pictured aboard the *St. Elmo*, which was the winner of the 1913 Walker Cup. The cup was sponsored by the Country Club of Detroit, which at the time was located in a lakefront clubhouse in Grosse Pointe. Sieder served as commodore of the Detroit Yacht Club in 1909 and 1910 and ran again in 1914, but lost to Harry Kendall. (HRC.)

When Harry Kendall campaigned for reelection as commodore in 1914, he did not own a sailboat. This might have been a liability if he had not already won 37 consecutive sailing races in his most famous boat, the *Shamrock*. After he was reelected, Kendall immediately purchased the *Puritana*, the 40-foot schooner pictured here. For the Detroit River Yacht-racing Association, he measured and inspected sailboats and served as chairman of the race committee. Kendall became such a presence that no race was considered official unless he was present and in charge. (LC.)

Detroit Yacht Club members began sailing catboats in 1898. The following year, the club bought its own fleet of five catboats. Prominent yachtsmen were concerned that catboats would breed a growing group of small-boat sailors who would not move up to big-boat sailing. But the large boats began to disappear, and catboats attracted more members. In 1924, the club owned eight catboats, and by 1927, had the largest fleet of privately owned catboats of any area yacht club. (WSU.)

DYC member Robert Oakman was one of the most experienced catboat skippers in the club when he began hosting an annual trophy event for catboats in 1924. Racing for the Oakman Trophy became the high point of the sailing season for small-boat sailors at the club. The race included club-owned catboats and catboats privately owned by DYC members. Sailors competed in three races on Lake St. Clair over a weekend. An awards dinner followed, and winners' names were inscribed on the solid silver trophy that was provided by Oakman. The Oakman Trophy is in the club's permanent collection. (WSU.)

This is the Detroit Yacht Club's 1930 Memorial Day regatta. The club's first Memorial Day regatta was for powerboats in 1901, because the West End Yacht Club, near Detroit's old Fort Wayne, claimed Memorial Day for its own sailboat regatta. The West End Yacht Club failed to hold the event in 1902, and the DYC started holding its annual Memorial Day regatta for sailboats in 1903. As the boats pictured here race, a dredge in the foreground is expanding Belle Isle. (WSU.)

The DYC Sailorettes met every week and worked to earn their skipper cards. In 1940, Doris Taylor became the first woman to receive a skipper's card. From left to right are (seated) Evelyn Welsh, Dorothy Trost, Betty Rypsam, Marge Behrens, Bea Block, Amy Williams, Genevieve Winckler, Sara Crampton, and Evelyn Rezenka behind Sara; (standing) Helen Huber, Ruth Warner, Bettie Downie, Dorothy "Dot" Christian, Eleanor Peacock, Helene McCracken, Faralyn Hunter, Doris Taylor, and Mary Ann Ward. (DYCC.)

Clete Welling's *Vitesse II* crew signal "V" for victory after winning the 1944 Port Huron to Mackinac Race. Carl Meurer is seated in the front. Behind him are, from left to right, Clarence Shaw, Avery Macklem, skipper Clete Welling, Dr. R. Dean "Doc" Ament, Ken Green (with pipe), Jim Armour, and Joe Snay. Welling was the first DYC skipper to win both the Mills Trophy, a premier sailing event on Lake Erie, and the Port Huron to Mackinac Race in the same year. (DYCC-CN.)

Clete Welling's *Vitesse II* raced in the 1946 DYC Memorial Day Regatta. *Vitesse II* and Toot Gmeiner's *Apache* were two of 20 yachts built for the New York Yacht Club in the 1930s. These sailboats were known as "New York 32s" since their length at the waterline was 32 feet. Welling and Gmeiner remained rivals for over 20 years, and each served as commodore of the Detroit Yacht Club, Welling in 1949 and Gmeiner in 1965. At one point in the 1980s, there were five New York 32s in the DYC harbor. (DYCC.)

The Gmeiner family are, from left to right, Nancy, Skip, Ruth, and Wilfred Toot Gmeiner aboard their sailboat *Apache*. Toot and his crew raced to victory on *Apache*, winning the Mills Trophy, the Inter-Lake Yachting Association championship, the Governor's Cup, and the Detroit Regional Yacht-racing Association championship. Gmeiner won the Port Huron to Mackinac Race five times. No Detroit Yacht Club member has ever won as many season championships on Lake St. Clair as Toot Gmeiner did with *Apache*, or equalled his five Port Huron to Mackinac wins. Both he and his son Skip served as DYC commodores. (GFC.)

Wilfred Toot Gmeiner (first row, second from left) is congratulated on July 27, 1959, after winning the Port Huron to Mackinac Race. Aboard *Apache*, Gmeiner hugged the shore almost the entire 235-mile route aboard his New York 32, winning an overall victory and the Cruising B title. (GFC.)

DYC past commodore Charles Sieder, right, aboard his cousin Dr. Harold Joerin's 36-foot yawl *El Chroma*, mends a sail with assistance from an unidentified helper in 1949. Commodore Sieder learned to work with canvas when he started working for J.C. Goss, a Detroit awning company. He later went into business for himself and made sails and then fabric tops for Ford convertibles. (HRC.)

Sitting on their sailboat *Blitzen* are, from left to right, Murray and Margaret Knapp and Ernie and Leona Grates. From 1944 to 1951, DYC members Ernie Grates and Murray Knapp won many races with the 55-foot *Blitzen*, including the Chicago to Mackinac Race in 1945 and 1946 and the Port Huron to Mackinac Race in 1945 and 1948. Their most memorable victory was the 1945 Port Huron to Mackinac Race, in which only 6 out of 40 boats finished. Knapp served as DYC commodore in 1951. (DYCC.)

DYC member Robert "Bob" Neesley can be seen in the stern as he steers his full gaff-rigged schooner *Malabar VI* in this 1951 photograph. Clem Carter is sitting on the side with his arm raised. Neesley's daughter Penny married Doug Breck and became a faithful DYC supporter for many years. She is the namesake of the club's Penny Breck award, given annually for outstanding contribution and service to the club by a female member. (HRC.)

"LAST STRAW"　　　　　D.R.Y.C. 1958 Class 'C' Champion

When DYC member Charles Buysee's 44-foot sloop *Last Straw* won the Toledo Yacht Club's Mills Trophy in 1946 on Lake Erie, it was the fifth straight year that a Detroit Yacht Club boat had won this event. When DYC members Jerry Clements and Clarence "Moon" Baker later owned *Last Straw*, they won Cruising A class honors in the Mills Trophy in 1958 and 1959, and were the overall winner in 1959. (DYCC.)

DYC members Clarence "Moon" Baker and Jerry Clements sold the *Last Straw* and bought the *X-Touche*, pictured here. Baker and Clements sailed *X-Touche* to win the 1960 Port Huron to Mackinac Race in their class. They also won the Mills Trophy in their classes from 1960 to 1962. Baker owned Baker's Keyboard Lounge, Detroit's premier jazz club, which featured well-known musicians such as Billie Holiday, Louis Armstrong, Ella Fitzgerald, Miles Davis, and Nat King Cole. (DYCC.)

Marilyn Jordan sits on the rail while skipper Eve Perry is at the tiller of a Flying Scot sailboat during the Sailorettes Annual Chairman's Race on Tuesday, August 13, 1968. The *Detroit Free Press* reported that on the day of the race, a female sailor was heard to remark that "the men don't make good crews." The race was won by Betty Nelson and Grace Fils. (DYCC.)

The Sailorettes pose before their annual tea on May 25, 1963. From left to right are Marilyn Jordan, Loretta Kaiser, Violet Wilson, Faralyn Hunter, Dorothy Christian, Joanne Estler, Genevieve Winckler, a Mrs. Butler, Vi Douglas, Alice Harris, Edna Donaldson, Rosemary Dorr, Helen Roth, Lucie Banta, Ruth Cherhan, Ethel Hemp, Peg Carey, Mary Hesse, Eve Perry, Wilma Bailey, Dorothy Trost, Rose Pearsall, and Germaine Dorr. (DYCC.)

DYC member Howard Riley and his crew aboard the *Tresor* finished first in their class in the 1996 Port Huron to Mackinac Race. Being the first to cross the finish line is difficult. But everyone can arrive at the Chippewa Hotel's Pink Pony Bar, which is commonly thought of as the second finish line. (HRC.)

After winning the Port Huron to Mackinac Race Shore Course PHRF Class N, the crew of the *Tresor* poses on July 16, 1996. From left to right are (first row) Bob Smahay, Sharon Riley, Jim Hammond, Jeannie Hammond, and Shannon Perry; (second row) Dwayne Looney, Paula Rocheleua, Howard Riley, Howard's son-in-law Carl Perry, Pam Harmount, Bob Harmount, Roland Day, Tony Lawrence, and Mark Szymanski. (HRC.)

The Detroit Yacht Club's fleet of Flying Scot sailboats are maintained for adult classes and class racing. The club also has Lasers, 420s, and Optimist dinghies for junior sailors. The DYC's Flying Scot sailing program includes sailing classes, races, and social activities. The DYC stopped using catboats and purchased its first Flying Scots in 1959. (DYCC-MS.)

In the foreground, DYC members Brien Baker and Mike Shields are sailing *Dynamis* in the Detroit River near the Renaissance Center. DYC members continue to compete successfully in sailboat races. Notable achievements include Baker and Shields's win of the Corinthian Trophy in the 2016 Port Huron to Mackinac Race. In the 2021 Port Huron to Mackinac Race, DYC member Tim LaRiviere, who races under the Bayview Yacht Club burgee, finished first, and Ed Bayer, Joel Kar, and Roy Lamphier, each in their own boats and class, finished second. (MCC.)

Robin Heller, president of the Detroit Yacht Club Foundation since 2021, is sailing aboard her yacht *Celebration*. She and her husband Bill and their children learned to sail in the Detroit Yacht Club's junior sailing program. As a junior sailor, Robin won the Detroit Regional Yacht-racing Association's Junior Girls' Championship in 1969 and 1970. She also raced in the national semifinal regatta for the Sears Cup. Her husband and her father have competed in the Port Huron to Mackinac Race. (HFC.)

Three

SPEEDBOAT RACING

When the Detroit Yacht Club moved onto Belle Isle, its focus began to change. A 1905 *Detroit Free Press* article quoted DYC commodore Otto Barthel: "Sailing yachts are now being supplanted by gasoline launches and while five years ago a good sailing regatta could always be had, today it is much easier to run a power boat regatta with a much larger number of entries."

The first world championship race for speedboats was held in 1903 for the British International Trophy, known as the Harmsworth Trophy. The race was established by England's Lord Northcutt. To compete for the Harmsworth Trophy, a boat had to be made of components found and manufactured in the nation that the boat represented. In 1904, the American Power Boat Association established the first Gold Cup race. Gas-powered engines were ascendant. Commodore Alex Mcleod, master sailor at the Detroit Yacht Club, bought his first motorboat in 1915. The newspapers stated, "Sailing Expert Bows to Progress."

When speedboat racing began, the sport was funded by wealthy individuals. Gar Wood epitomized this early period. He loved competition and considered it a mechanic's game. An inventor, he could afford whatever he could imagine. He used four Packard engines in one boat to set a world speed record of 125 miles per hour. Gar Wood won the Gold Cup five times and the Harmsworth Trophy seven times.

An Internal Revenue Service ruling in 1963 allowed racing teams to claim a deduction for operating expenses, and speedboat racing changed significantly. Racing was no longer the exclusive pursuit of wealthy sportsmen. To enter the Gold Cup, contestants no longer had to belong to a yacht club—it became a commercial enterprise. Speedboats now had corporate sponsorships and displayed commercial decals. And the boats changed. The fastest boats were now powered by Vietnam-era helicopter turbine engines.

It became an age of modern unlimited hydroplanes. They could travel above the water at over 200 miles per hour on a cushion of air, connected to the water at only three points. A new era had begun.

DYC member Oliver Barthel, front left in the *Six Shooter*, managed all of the early speedboat races for the Detroit Yacht Club. At the time, 12 miles per hour was considered fast, but the *Six Shooter* was twice that at 25 miles per hour. Its two brass exhaust pipes sat atop the hogback deck, and with no muffler, the noise and the speed left onlookers amazed. The original bridge to Belle Isle is in the background. (NAHC.)

Oliver E. Barthel, front left, and W.T. Norton, skipper, right, are seated in the *Six Shooter*. When the six-cylinder, 70-horsepower engine was first installed at Olds Motor Works in 1905, it did not operate for more than 15 minutes before stopping. Olds factory engineers were unable to fix the problem, and asked Barthel for help. He redesigned the cylinder block and rebuilt the engine, solving the problem. Oliver's brother Otto Barthel served as commodore of the Detroit Yacht Club in 1906 and 1925. (NAHC.)

The Hotel Pontchartrain stood at the corner of Cadillac Square and Woodward Avenue and was where people met for dealmaking. Chris Smith, who later co-founded the Chris-Craft company, built *Baby Speed Demon II*, which won the 1914 Gold Cup. Smith needed $10,000 to build his next Gold Cup speedboat. At the hotel, he helped form the Miss Detroit Powerboat Association, led by DYC members Gus Schantz, Horace Dodge Sr., and William Metzger. Together, they raised money to build *Miss Detroit*. They appealed to civic pride and sold certificates of membership in the association to the public. Smith built *Miss Detroit* and placed it on display in the lobby of the Hotel Pontchartrain to help with fundraising. (WSU.)

Miss Detroit raced on Long Island's Manhasset Bay and won the 1915 Gold Cup. Detroit citizens, with the encouragement of Mayor Oscar Marx, loved the idea of a boat representing their city and raised most of the money needed to build *Miss Detroit*. The win assured that the Miss Detroit Powerboat Association would hold the 1916 Gold Cup in front of the Detroit Yacht Club. (LC.)

Miss Minneapolis won the 1916 Gold Cup. This boat was built by Chris Smith for the Minneapolis Boat Club. The Miss Detroit Powerboat Association wanted Smith to build a new boat for them, but still owed him $1,800 from the 1915 race. At a 1916 Detroit Exchange Club luncheon, organizers asked if there was a loyal Detroiter present who would buy *Miss Detroit* and settle the debt. A new man in town named Gar Wood offered $1,000 cash and a six-month note for the balance. His offer was accepted. (MNHS.)

Gar Wood not only bought *Miss Detroit*, he also bought a controlling interest in Chris Smith's Boat and Engine Company's boatyard in Algonac, Michigan. Smith built *Miss Detroit II*, and Wood won the 1917 Gold Cup in Minneapolis. Wood's victory meant that the Gold Cup would again be held at Detroit in 1918. Smith built five *Miss Detroits* and the first two *Miss Americas* that Gar Wood used to win the Gold Cup and the Harmsworth Trophy. In this 1920s photograph, Wood, left, and his mechanic Orlin Johnson appear in their racing suits. Later, in 1922, Chris Smith and his sons sold their remaining interest in the boatyard to Gar Wood. Then Smith formed a new business, Chris Smith and Sons Boat Company, which became the world's largest builder of motorboats and was eventually renamed Chris-Craft. (DHS.)

Gar Wood kept winning races. In 1920, he entered the British International Trophy for Motor Boats, known as the Harmsworth Trophy. He spent $250,000 to have Chris Smith build two different boats. The *Miss Detroit V* was 38 feet long and built for rough water, and the *Miss America* was 26 feet long and made for calm water. He took both to England. Wood, left, and Chris Smith's son Jay Smith, in the *Miss America*, won the 1920 Harmsworth Trophy. (WSU.)

Detroit was ecstatic that Gar Wood beat the British and brought the Harmsworth Trophy to America. His parade must have looked as good as this 1919 parade on Woodward Avenue. Wood received the keys to the city and was paraded down Woodward Avenue with a police escort and the Dodge Brothers band before thousands of spectators. At the waterfront, Wood and his wife, Murlen, boarded a yacht that went upstream to the Detroit Yacht Club. All along the shoreline people cheered, factory whistles blew, and fireboats sprayed water high in the air. (WSU.)

Commodore Gar Wood, with his son in arms, watches as his wife, Murlen, christens his new boat, *Miss America II*, two weeks before the September 5, 1921, Harmsworth Trophy. DYC members witnessed the christening at Commodore Alex McLeod's summer home in Algonac, Michigan. *Miss America II*, like all of Wood's boats, were single-step hydroplanes that had a notch in the keel, making the boats plane above the water. Gar Wood won the race. (DHS.)

DYC member Charles Ross's cruiser *Susanne* finished third in the Sallan Trophy at the 1921 Gold Cup Regatta. The regatta included races for the Detroit Trophy, the Great Lakes Trophy, the Sallan Trophy, the Scripps Motor Company Trophy, the Wood-Fisher Trophy, the Gold Cup, and the Harmsworth Trophy. Gar Wood, driving *Miss America II*, not only won the Harmsworth Trophy at the regatta, but also won the Gold Cup for the fifth year in a row. In the background is the Detroit Yacht Club's 1905 Belle Isle clubhouse. (HRC.)

The Yachtsmen's Association of America (YAA) was organized in 1922. From left to right are W.D. "Eddie" Edenburn, Arthur Bray, J. Lee Barrett holding the burgee, unidentified, and Commodore Gus Schantz. The YAA was formed in reaction to a rule change for the Gold Cup. The American Power Boat Association was unhappy that Gar Wood kept winning it, and wanted the Gold Cup returned to New York. So, the association banned single-step hydroplanes and motors larger than 625 cubic inches, which eliminated Wood from Gold Cup races. (DHS.)

This is the Detroit Yacht Club's 1925 Labor Day Regatta. The YAA became the official authority representing the United States for the Harmsworth Trophy and other international speedboat races. It held its first 150-mile International Sweepstakes race on Labor Day in 1923. The race consisted of 50 laps on a three-mile course on the Detroit River. Edsel Ford, vice commodore of the YAA, sent the Ford Motor Company's 57-piece band to perform at that regatta, seen here in the foreground. (WSU.)

On September 5, 1925, Delphine Dodge Cromwell became the first woman to win a speedboat race at the Detroit Yacht Club. She was warned that it was too dangerous for a woman to risk being in a speedboat race. Cromwell refused to act according to expectations. She rode as the mechanic, sitting next to the driver, because she wanted to prove to her brother that she was not afraid to race in a speedboat. (DHS.)

ASSOCIATED NEWS SERVICE
LATEST WORLD EVENTS IN PICTURES

"NUISANCE" WINS DETROIT REGATTA
Start of the annual Christcraft Invitation Race, Detroit, which was won by Mrs. Delphine Dodge Cromwell (inset) in her speed boat, "Nuisance." Second place went to her brother, Horace Dodge, driving "Solar Plexus."

Commodore Gar Wood, in his *Baby Gar IV*, races past Miami Beach's Fleetwood Hotel to win the Fisher-Allison Trophy in 1925. Many Detroit Yacht Club members who wintered in Florida stayed here. Others, like Robert and Mamie Oakman, stayed at the Flamingo Hotel. There were even those who had their yachts brought south and lived on them for the winter season. (HMM.)

Here is a look at the DYC main dock in 1926. In the upper left is the two-story barge that served as the judges' stand for races. Sportswriters were assigned to the lower deck, and judges were on the top deck. That year, T.A. Clarke, representing France, challenged Gar Wood for the Harmsworth Trophy. Clarke's wife demanded to sit on the barge to watch her husband race. No woman had been allowed this privilege before, but Mrs. Clarke was not to be denied, and watched the race from the top deck of the barge. (BGSU-CAC.)

Thousands of spectators wait on shore and in boats for the 1926 race to start. The French challenger, *Excelsior*, far right, lined up with Gar Wood's three boats, from left to right, *Miss America IV, Miss America V,* and *Miss America III. Excelsior's* engine trouble delayed the race for hours. Wood's men eventually towed the *Excelsior* around the river until its engines started. When Clarke finally got to the starting line, his boat went a half mile before the engines died. The race was over. Gar Wood, in *Miss America V,* won the Harmsworth Trophy for a third time. (DHS.)

Count and Countess Johnston-Noad, left, and Frederick Cooper, right, arrived in Detroit from Britain for the 1927 Yachtsmen's Association of America 150-mile International Sweepstakes race. Although there were no Harmsworth or Gold Cup races at the Detroit Yacht Club that year, rich and famous speedboat racers still came from Canada, Great Britain, and Germany for this YAA race. (WSU.)

Pictured is the main dock in 1927. At the end of the dock is the permanent judges' stand that replaced the double-decker barge. Gus Schantz and his committee arranged for the first military flyover for a Detroit Yacht Club regatta. After the flyover, the planes flew in formation around the regatta course at 150 miles per hour under the command of Maj. Thomas G. Lanphier. (WSU.)

The 1927 judges' platform at the end of the main dock is seen from the river. DYC speedboat races began with a flying start, so timing was crucial. The set of five discs at the top of the platform told drivers when the race had started. A gun would signal that in one minute the first disc would drop, and every minute thereafter, another would fall. The challenge was to cross the starting line at the right time. These discs have all dropped, so this race was already underway. (WSU.)

Miss America VII was built in 13 days following the disintegration of Miss America VI while going 98 miles per hour during a trial run. Gar Wood almost drowned, and Orlin Johnson nearly died, his throat cut almost ear to ear. Wood and Johnson surfaced in a pool of blood. When Johnson regained consciousness, he remarked, "Guess we'll have to build another boat." After four days, Wood found his engines at the bottom of the river. Johnson got out of the hospital, and with Wood, beat Marion Carstairs and won the Harmsworth Trophy on September 1, 1928. (DHS.)

Enjoying a good laugh are, from left to right, Marion Carstairs and Murlen and Gar Wood on September 5, 1931. Carstairs returned to Detroit from England that year to support her countryman Kaye Don when he challenged Wood for the Harmsworth Trophy. A Standard Oil heiress, Carstairs spent over $500,000 trying to beat Wood in Harmsworth Trophy races, but lost to him in 1928, 1929, and 1930. Carstairs decided that she had spent enough money and quit racing Wood. (AP.)

Three boats pass the judges' stand in a flying start, with Kaye Don's *Miss England II* in the lead on September 6, 1931. Gar Wood's boat, *Miss America IX*, is nearest to the dock. His other boat, *Miss America VIII*, is piloted by his brother George Wood. Don's boat had two Rolls-Royce engines providing 4,000 horsepower, and *Miss America IX* had two Packard engines delivering 2,800 horsepower. Kaye Don won this first heat of the Harmsworth Trophy. It was the first heat Gar Wood ever lost in a Harmsworth race. (WSU.)

Spectators and cars jam the shoreline for the Dodge Sweepstakes race, which took place immediately before the Harmsworth race on September 7, 1931. That gave Gar Wood and Orlin Johnson time to jump into *Miss America IX* and take off from Wood's upstream Grayhaven home with a flying start. Both Wood and Don jumped the clock, crossed the starting line early, and were disqualified. Wood's brother George won the second and third heats while racing *Miss America VIII*. He won the Harmsworth Trophy, which remained at the Detroit Yacht Club. (WSU.)

Gar Wood, left, and Orlin Johnson are prepared for Kaye Don's second challenge for the Harmsworth Trophy in 1932. Their new boat, *Miss America X*, held 300 gallons of gas, weighed seven and a half tons, and had four 12-cylinder Packard engines delivering 7,600 horsepower. Wood defeated Don again. The last challenge by the British for the Harmsworth Trophy was mounted by Britain's Hubert Scott-Paine in 1933. Wood won that race also. (DYCC.)

Gar Wood's home, just upstream from the Detroit Yacht Club, is the large white building with the four chimneys. He also had homes in Algonac, Michigan; Georgian Bay, Canada; Honolulu, Hawaii; and Miami Beach, Florida. At upper right, just across the Grayhaven Canal from Wood's 40-room mansion, was DYC member Charles Fisher's Lenox Street home. Both houses are gone now; Wood's mansion was replaced by new homes and condominiums. (WSU.)

Gar Wood's boatbuilding factory, seen here, was in Algonac, Michigan. His technical ability, inventor's keenness, and personal fortune enabled him to continue building the next speedboat. He patented and manufactured the hydraulic hoist for dump trucks. The hoists were used by thousands of trucks and gave Wood an estimated fortune of $50 million. According to the *Detroit News*, Gar Wood Industries made money even during the Depression. (WSU.)

Biscayne Bay, Florida, was the site of many winning races for Gar Wood in the 1920s. DYC member Herbert Mendelsohn's *Madoshumi V*, driven by Clell Perry, won here in 1934 and 1935. The Fleetwood Hotel, center, was popular with Detroit Yacht Club members in the 1920s and 1930s. Wood was not the only DYC member to race at Biscayne Bay, just the most famous. (WSU.)

Pres. Franklin Roosevelt presents Herbert Mendelsohn with a medal for winning the 1937 President's Cup. On the Oval Office desk is the President's Cup trophy. Clell Perry, driver of the winning boat, the *Notre Dame*, is on the right with his hands clasped. Mendelson's boats also won the Gold Cup in 1937 and the President's Cup in 1935 and 1940. President's Cup races were not held from 1941 to 1945 due to gasoline rationing during World War II. (LC.)

At the White House, Pres. Harry Truman, center, shakes hands with Danny Foster, the 1947 President's Cup winner. Foster drove *Miss Peps V*, which was owned by Detroit Yacht Club members Roy, Russell, and Walter Dossin. Roy Dossin is to the right of Foster, and his brother Walter is behind him. The Dossin brothers were from Detroit and owned the largest Pepsi-Cola bottler in the nation. They sponsored four boats between 1946 and 1956 and enjoyed considerable success. (DHS.)

From left to right, Detroit Yacht Club members Walter, Russell, and Roy Dossin stand behind their trophies. Their hydroplane *Miss Peps V* defeated Guy Lombardo's *Tempo VI* in Jamaica Bay on Long Island Sound and returned the Gold Cup to Detroit in 1947. The Dossins' later boat, *Miss Pepsi*, is considered the greatest of all step hydroplanes and won the Silver Cup in 1951 and the President's Cup in 1950, 1951, and 1952. *Miss Pepsi* remains on permanent display at the Dossin Great Lakes Museum on Belle Isle. (DHS.)

Guy Lombardo, left, stands in his boat *Tempo VI* with DYC member Jack Schaefer Sr., who owned Schaefer Bakery. Lombardo loved racing hydroplanes and won the 1946 Gold Cup and the 1955 Silver Cup at the Detroit Yacht Club. He owned several hydroplanes and named them all *Such Crust*. Schaefer's best year was 1948, when he won the President's Cup. (DHS.)

Guy Lombardo, left, and Lou Fageol celebrate their victories at the Detroit Yacht Club's 1946 Labor Day awards ceremony. Lombardo won the Gold Cup, and Fageol won the Silver Cup. The Silver Cup race was composed of Gold Cup starters who were eliminated after the first Gold Cup heat. It was awarded annually from 1946 through 1961. John Mulford, far right, donated the Silver Cup to the DYC in memory of his father, O.J. Mulford, a DYC regatta official. In 1964, Guy Lombardo and his orchestra, the Royal Canadians, played for a dance at the club. (WSU.)

Detroit Yacht Club member John Hacker, standing by the car with his hands on his hips, is looking at *My Sweetie*, a boat he designed. Hacker was trained as a marine architect and was known for the superior finishes, fittings, and elegant designs of his mahogany Hackercraft boats. Not only did he design beautiful boats for the public, ut he also designed winning hydroplanes for racers. Hacker's Gold Cup winners were *El Lagarto* in 1933, 1934, and 1935, and *My Sweetie* in 1949. He also designed the Dossin brothers' 1950 *Miss Pepsi*, which won three national championships. (DHS.)

Detroit Yacht Club member Albin "Al" Fallon, center, is at a drivers' meeting at Kean's Yacht Harbor in 1950. Meetings of owners and drivers preceded every race. Fallon was the president of Great Lakes Broach and Gage Company in Detroit. He owned *Miss Great Lakes*, a three-point hydroplane that was powered by a surplus World War II Allison aircraft engine. Danny Foster drove *Miss Great Lakes* for Fallon and won the President's Cup in 1946 and the Detroit Gold Cup in 1948. (DHS.)

DYC member Horace Dodge Jr. celebrates the victory of his boat My *Sweetie Dora*, which won the 1954 Silver Cup. Enjoying the awards ceremony at the Detroit Yacht Club are, from left to right, his mother, Anna Thompson Dodge (seated); Suzy Mulford, pouring champagne into the Silver Cup; Dodge, standing behind his wife, Gregg; and Jack Bartlow, the driver of My *Sweetie Dora*. Dodge is credited with helping to keep the American Power Boat Association's Gold Cup races alive during the Depression, when he spent millions maintaining crews and boats. (DHS.)

Horace Dodge Jr., his hand on the trophy, is next to Jack Bartlow, the driver of My *Sweetie Dora*. They both enjoyed drinking champagne from the Silver Cup. The onlookers, including two commodores wearing their race ribbons, were gathered on the broad outdoor staircase that rose from the river side of the clubhouse to its second floor. Dodge entered more boats in Gold Cup races than anyone else and won the Gold Cup in 1932 and 1936. (DHS.)

The Horace Dodge Memorial Racing Pits in Waterworks Park were built in 1966 for launching hydroplanes. The facility was paid for by Anna Thompson Dodge in memory of her son Horace Dodge Jr., who died in 1963. She donated $150,000 to have the pits constructed. Here, cranes are lowering hydroplanes into the water in preparation for a race. The Roostertail in the background was built by Joe Schoenith to overlook a turn in the DYC racecourse. It gets its name from the 50-foot spray of water thrown in the air behind the hydroplanes. (DHS.)

The new Gar Wood Judges Stand was built across the river from the Detroit Yacht Club in 1959. Wood attended the ceremonial groundbreaking in March, and the stand was finished in time for the Fourth of July Detroit Memorial Regatta. He donated $50,000, and the City of Detroit provided the land. It was a final gift to Detroit from Wood, who for years drew hundreds of thousands of people to the Detroit River to watch the best powerboat racing in the world. (DHS.)

The Gale racing team members are, from left to right, Bill Cantrell, DYC member Joe Schoenith, and Joe's son Lee. The team was named for Schoenith's W.D. Gale Electric Company. Between 1950 and 1972, the team won two Gold Cups and four national championships from the American Power Boat Association. Hydroplane racing on the Detroit River was placed in doubt in 1962 due to inadequate financial support. Schoenith and his business friend Jack Adams stepped forward and organized the Spirit of Detroit Association, which funded hydroplane races on the river until 2002. (DHS.)

Detroit Yacht Club member George Simon started racing in 1953 and named his hydroplanes *Miss U.S.* after his company, the US Equipment Company. The shape of a hydroplane makes the air go slower over the top of the boat, which lifts the bottom, causing the boat to ride on a cushion of air. Hydroplanes travel at 200 miles per hour. Simon promised his wife that if he ever won the Gold Cup, he would quit racing. He won the 1976 Gold Cup and quit. (DHS.)

In the foreground is the hydroplane *Miss DYC* racing past the DYC clubhouse. *Miss DYC* was sponsored by the Detroit Yacht Club and the Dick Scott Automotive Group. *Miss DYC* beat the reigning champion, Anheuser-Busch's *Miss Budweiser*, and won the 2004 Gold Cup. The DYC has sponsored other hydroplanes, hosted an annual Gold Cup Gala, served as a presenting sponsor of the Gold Cup in 2011 and 2012, and was the title sponsor of the Gold Cup in 2013. (FPW.)

Miss DYC was placed on display at the Detroit Yacht Club during the 2004 Gold Cup Regatta. DYC member Mark Weber and his wife, Lori, are pictured in front of *Miss DYC*. At age 15, Weber was going 90 miles per hour on the river before he was old enough to drive a car. He won the American Power Boat Association national championship 14 times. Weber served as president of the American Power Boat Association and is president of Detroit Riverfront Events Incorporated, which organizes the Detroit Hydrofest hydroplane races on the river. (MWC.)

Four

THE AUTO INDUSTRY
AND THE DYC

When the Detroit Yacht Club moved from McDougall Street to the Park House Hotel in 1891 (near present-day Indian Village), it actually left the city limits of Detroit. The horse-drawn streetcar line on East Jefferson Avenue did not extend to the club's new location. This lack of reliable public transportation was an inconvenience to club members.

The momentous change from horse-drawn streetcars to the convenience of personal automobiles happened over the course of 20 years. What this would mean for Detroit's industry and the Detroit Yacht Club could not be imagined at the time. Jay Cooley, an 1897 investor in Detroit's first automobile factory, the Oldsmobile Motor Works, remarked he did not have the faintest idea of what the automobile business would become.

Detroit's industry leaders remade the riverfront with factories. The Oldsmobile Motor Works built its factory on the Detroit River in 1899, adjacent to the Belle Isle Bridge. The industrialization of the riverfront meant more factories, more jobs, and a busier Detroit River. The factories and the commercial river traffic were crowding out the rowing, canoeing, and sailing clubs.

Many DYC members were connected to the automotive industry. Between 1900 and 1930, the sixfold increase in Detroit's population, from 305,000 to 1,837,000, was a direct result of Detroit's ascendance as the automotive capital of the world. By 1925, over 225,000 men were employed in Detroit's 79 automobile factories and automobile accessory plants. It is not surprising that members of the automotive industry, from executives to factory supervisors, have always been a significant portion of the Detroit Yacht Club's membership.

In 1896, Oliver Barthel, left, and Charles Brady King drive Detroit's first gas-propelled automobile on the streets. They built the car together. Barthel was an engineer who worked in Detroit's early automotive industry, for both Ransom E. Olds and Henry Ford. He was also the first engineer for the Cadillac Motor Car Company. He and his brother Otto Barthel were members of the Detroit Yacht Club. Otto served as commodore in 1906 and 1925 and was a patent attorney closely identified with the automobile industry. (NAHC.)

Detroit Yacht Club member Ransom E. Olds, shown on his yacht *Reomar IV*, loved boating. He built Detroit's first factory for the production of automobiles in 1899. A 1901 fire destroyed most of it, but a prototype of the curved-dash Oldsmobile survived. Once in production, this model became very popular. In 1904, Olds moved to Lansing, Michigan, and started the Reo Motor Car Company, but he remained a member of the Detroit Yacht Club into the 1940s. As the owner of the first automobile factory in Michigan, he is considered the founder of Michigan's automobile industry. (OFA-SF.)

Detroit Yacht Club member William Metzger helped organize the Cadillac Motor Car Company in 1902. He sold it three years later and started the Northern Motor Car Company, which became the E-M-F Company, whose name was derived from the founders' surnames—Barney Everitt, William Metzger, and Walter Flanders. The company was ultimately purchased by the Studebaker Corporation. Metzger was the treasurer of the Miss Detroit Powerboat Association and raised the money to send the *Miss Detroit* to the 1915 Gold Cup in New York. (BHC.)

Detroit Yacht Club member Henry B. Joy, left, sits in the driver's seat next to Fredrick M. Alger in a 1907 Packard roadster. In his career at the Packard Motor Car Company, Joy began as a general manager in 1903, rose to president, and retired as chairman of the board in 1918. Joy was instrumental in moving the Packard factory from Ohio to Detroit. Packard was the most popular luxury car of the 1920s and early 1930s. (NAHC.)

In 1905, Alex McLeod was both the commodore of the Detroit Yacht Club and the president and general manager of the Maxwell-Briscoe-McLeod Automobile Company. He served as the first president of the Detroit Auto Dealers Association, founded in 1907, and was the chief executive of its auto show that year. The Maxwell-Briscoe-McLeod Automobile Company evolved into the Maxwell Automobile Company, which was reorganized by Walter Chrysler and became part of the Chrysler Corporation in 1925. (DYCC.)

Detroit Yacht Club member Horace Dodge Sr. owned the yacht *Nokomis*, pictured her. The ship was 154 feet long and carried a crew of 20. Horace and his brother John Dodge were original stockholders of the Ford Motor Company and supplied Ford with engines, transmissions, axles, and chassis for 10 years. In 1914, they started the Dodge Brothers Motor Car Company, and within a few years, their plant ranked fourth in the country in the production of automobiles. (AOM.)

Nokomis served as the judges' boat for the Gold Cup in 1916. The Dodge brothers surrendered it to the US Navy for military use during World War I. On the final cruise of *Nokomis* were, from left to right, John Dodge, Andolph Vocell, Albert Andrich, unidentified, Robert Oakman, Edward Fitzgerald, Horace Dodge Sr., and Detroit mayor Oscar Marx. Horace Dodge Sr. was elected fleet captain of the Detroit Yacht Club in 1918. (AOM.)

The *Delphine* was the last ship built for Horace Dodge Sr. It was the largest private yacht on the Great Lakes and measured 258 feet long and weighed 1,225 tons. The yacht had a stateroom for the owner, nine guest rooms, and a crew of 60. Horace Dodge Sr. died in 1920 before the *Delphine* was finished, and his wife, Anna Dodge, had the ship completed. She kept it in his memory for the remainder of her life. The *Delphine* is passing under the Bluewater Bridge connecting Port Huron to Canada in this late 1930s photograph. (BGSU-HC.)

Mayor James Couzens, standing on the cornerstone of the future DYC clubhouse, was a member of the Detroit Yacht Club and one of the richest men in the nation. In 1903, he joined the newly formed Ford Motor Company. He was a genius in management and finance and for many years helped Henry Ford manufacture the Model T, the most popular automobile in America. Determined to try a new challenge, Couzens resigned from the company in 1915, entered politics, and in 1918, was elected mayor of Detroit. (WSU.)

Detroit Yacht Club member W.D. "Eddie" Edenburn was a human dynamo. He officiated at the first 19 Indianapolis 500 races, worked for the American Automobile Association, and was the automotive editor and assistant sports editor for the *Detroit News*. Edenburn worked on the Detroit Yacht Club's Gold Cup race committee from 1918 to 1933. (DYCC.)

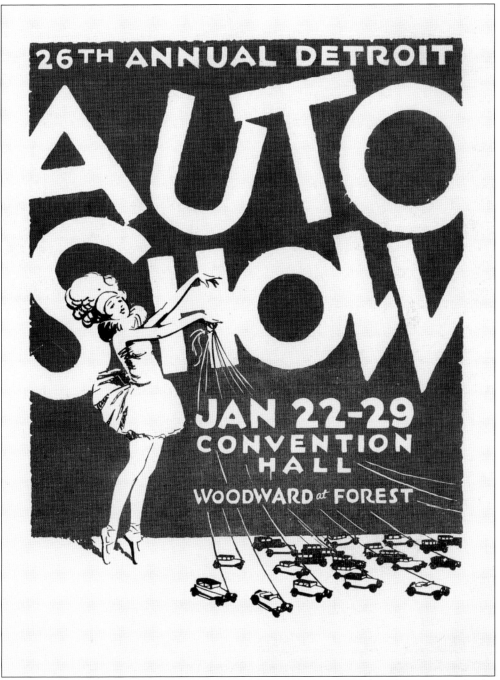

Eddie Edenburn also served as the manager of the Detroit Auto Dealers Association. As the publisher of the *Mainsheet*, the DYC's monthly magazine, Edenburn arranged for this auto show advertisement to be placed in the January 1927 issue. Club members loved and revered Edenburn. (DYCC.)

Detroit Yacht Club member Edsel Ford, background, with his wife, Eleanor, are onboard one of their boats. Ford became president of the Ford Motor Company in 1919 and joined the Detroit Yacht Club in April 1921. He served as vice commodore of both the Detroit Gold Cup race committee and the Yachtsmen's Association of America. (THF.)

Here, Edsel Ford drives *Nine-Ninety-Nine* past the Ford River Rouge Industrial Complex in 1923. Ford owned sailboats and speedboats and set a world record driving his speedboat the *Woodfish* in 1922. He entered his speedboats *Woodfish*, *Goldfish*, *Greyhound Jr.*, and *Nine-Ninety-Nine* in the 1923 Gold Cup at the Detroit Yacht Club. Paul Strasburg drove *Woodfish* and finished in first place to win the William J. Siebert Trophy in the 15-mile free-for-all race. He also finished fourth in the Yachtsmen's Association of America 150-mile International Sweepstakes race. (THF.)

Henry Ford owned the steam yacht *Sialia* when he joined the Detroit Yacht Club in 1923. Two years later, Ford had the Detroit Shipbuilding Company cut *Sialia* in half and begin the process of removing the steam plant to install diesel engines. He also lengthened the yacht by 21 feet. The work was completed in time for Ford to participate in the Detroit Yacht Club's Venetian Night festivities on September 3, 1925. (THF.)

The Defoe Shipbuilding Company built the *Rosewill* for DYC member William Rand in 1926. Rand bought out the Wheeler Manufacturing Company in 1903 and began producing windshields, automobile tops, and lamp brackets for the automobile industry. In 1916, he combined six companies into the Motor Products Corporation with a capitalization of $10 million. By 1931, Rand's company was providing parts for almost every important automobile manufacturer. (BGSU-HC.)

Odis Porter, left, and Detroit Yacht Club member Chester "Chet" Ricker are clocking Gar Wood the day he drove *Miss America X* at 125 nautical miles per hour on September 20, 1932. Porter and Ricker were the official timers at the Detroit Yacht Club and at the Indianapolis 500 races. Ricker was also a freelance automotive technical writer and president of Day-Nite Company, which manufactured his patented automobile headlight fixtures. (WSU.)

Detroit Yacht Club member Charles Kettering's new yacht, the *Olive K II*, was launched on September 5, 1929. Kettering ordered the yacht the day after Alfred P. Sloan and Fred J. Fisher, president and vice president of General Motors, announced they had ordered new yachts. Kettering had Defoe Boat and Motor Works in Bay City, Michigan, include a still in his yacht. To remain within the law, the still was registered for scientific purposes with the US Treasury Department. (DHS.)

Pictured here from left to right are Edsel and Henry Ford and William Mayo. Henry Ford built one of the first modern airports in the nation in 1924, and Edsel promoted aviation with the Air Reliability Tour. William Mayo was the chief power engineer and head of aviation for Ford Motor Company. All were members of the Detroit Yacht Club. Mayo hosted Charles and Anne Lindbergh aboard his yacht *Rhula* to watch the 1930 Harmsworth Race at the Detroit Yacht Club. (WSU.)

Detroit Yacht Club member Albert Kahn examines a blueprint in his studio. Kahn designed the Ford Motor Company Highland Park Plant and River Rouge complex. He designed Ford assembly plants across the United States and automotive factories for Hudson, Packard, Chrysler, and General Motors. Kahn's iconic landmarks include Detroit's Fisher Building, the General Motors Building, and the Grosse Pointe Shores home of Edsel Ford. (WSU.)

The seven Fisher brothers and their mother, Margaret Fisher, celebrate her 79th birthday in 1936. From left to right are (seated) Edward, Margaret, and Howard; (standing) William, Frederick, Charles, Alfred, and Lawrence. Charles and Frederick Fisher and their uncle Albert Fisher formed the Fisher Body Company in 1908. By 1912, the company was building 100,000 car bodies a year. In 1910, the Fisher brothers sold a three-fifths interest in their company to the General Motors Corporation. Alfred, Charles, Edward, Lawrence, and William were members of the Detroit Yacht Club. (DHS.)

Charles Fisher's steel yacht *Saramar III* (pictured) was built by the Defoe Shipbuilding Company in 1930. William Fisher owned the *Laura M. IV*, and Lawrence Fisher owned the *Margaret III*. After the General Motors Corporation bought the remainder of the Fisher Body Company in 1926, six of the seven brothers went on to serve as a vice president for General Motors. (BGSU-HC.)

Detroit Yacht Club member Bill Fisher, left, son of Charles Fisher, talks to Russell Alger III before they compete in the Port Huron to Mackinac Race on July 21, 1934. The previous year, Fisher and his crew, aboard the *Margaret F IV*, beat Alger's *Baccarat* in a match race on Memorial Day at the Detroit Yacht Club. It was thought that Fisher had a chance to beat Alger in the 1933 Port Huron to Mackinac Race, but he lost to him in both 1933 and 1934. (WSU.)

Celebrating Chris Sinsabaugh's 64th birthday party at Detroit's Recess Club, are, from left to right, Harlow Curtice, president of Buick Motor Company; Chris Sinsabaugh, editor at *Automotive Daily News*; Charles Kettering; and Kaufman Keller, president of the Chrysler Corporation. Kettering was the Detroit Yacht Club's commodore and the president of the General Motors Research Laboratories in 1934. Known as "Boss Kett," he was in charge of research for 27 years and held 186 US patents. Kettering retired with approximately $33 million in General Motors stock, and together with Alfred Sloan, created the Sloan-Kettering Institute in 1945. (DHS.)

Walter Briggs, owner of the Detroit Tigers, sits in Tiger Stadium on June 24, 1938. He owned Briggs Manufacturing Company and supplied car bodies to Chrysler, Stutz, Packard, Pierce-Arrow, and Lincoln. A Detroit Yacht Club member, Briggs owned the steel yacht *Cambronia*, the sister ship to Alfred P. Sloan's *Rene* and Frederick Fisher's *Nakhoda*. The *Cambronia* had an overall length of 236 feet and a rated speed of 17 knots. (EHSC.)

At the Ford Willow Run bomber plant on June 12, 1942, are, from left to right, Charles E. Sorensen, Lt. Gen. William S. Knudsen, and Edsel Ford. Sorensen was vice president and general manager of Ford Motor Company. Building the plant that produced B-24 bombers on a moving assembly line was Sorensen's crowning achievement. In 1927, he was the commodore of the Detroit Yacht Club, and his new 105-foot all-steel ocean cruiser *Helene* was the club's flagship that year. (BHC.)

Joseph Galamb, a Detroit Yacht Club member, sits in his office at the Ford Motor Company in 1943. Galamb was a mechanical engineer who left Hungary and made his way to Detroit in 1903. He began working for the Ford Motor Company in 1905 and worked directly with Henry Ford to create the revolutionary design for the Model T. He later worked on the Model A, tractors, and experimental engines. In 1944, Galamb retired after 39 years at Ford. (THF.)

DYC member Fred W. Rypsam, left, shares his knowledge with John Tompkins. Rypsam was one of more than 1,000 Detroit residents who earned a living as a commercial artist. He worked for the Studebaker Corporation and then the Studebaker-Packard Corporation. By 1947, Detroit was the center for commercial artists for the automotive industry. Tompkins grew up at the club. His father, C.S. Tompkins, was the commodore in 1958, and John served as commodore in 2021. (DYCC.)

DYC member Charles Wellar, right, eats lunch with his grandnephew Ed Theisen Jr. at the Detroit Yacht Club in 1952. Wellar worked from 1905 to 1951 at Great Lakes Steel in Ecorse, Michigan. In 1931, Great Lakes Steel provided 400 tons of steel daily to the Murray Corporation of America. Murray's heavy stamping division fabricated the steel into car and truck chassis frames. Wellar retired from Great Lakes Steel as the yard master in 1951. His grandnephew served as commodore of the Detroit Yacht Club in 1989. (ETC.)

Five

ART AND ARTIFACTS

The Detroit Yacht Club building was designed by the George D. Mason Company in the Spanish Colonial Revival style. The Mediterranean architectural elements include exterior stucco walls, balconies, verandas with ornamental ironwork, and a low pitched roof clad in glazed clay tile.

The club's main entrance is outlined by stonework and is crowned with a lintel bearing the face of Neptune, who peers down on all who approach his domain. The interior includes balustrades and coffered ceilings. The second-floor lobby has an opaline glass ceiling set in a wrought iron frame. Ceiling beams in the ballroom and East Lounge are stenciled with polychrome decorations, and sea creatures adorn the ceiling of the Fountain Room.

The Trophy Room displays the club's permanent collection of trophies. Every trophy has a story. For example, it was unusual the first time freshwater sailors beat saltwater sailors at the annual Miami to Nassau Race, but it happened. DYC members Ernie Grates and Murray Knapp, with their Detroit crew aboard *Blitzen*, won the race for the third time in 1950 and brought the Nassau Cup home. It is now in the DYC Trophy Room. And then there is the 1894 Detroit Mayor Hazen Pingree Sailing Trophy. It was the club's oldest perpetual trophy when it was accidentally lost in the lagoon after the 1983 Memorial Day Regatta. After several attempts at recovery, the trophy was never found. A replacement is now in the Trophy Room.

A variety of art graces the walls and rooms of the clubhouse. Chandeliers from Anna Dodge's Rose Terrace estate light Peacock Alley. Pewabic tile depicting a seagull in flight greets those who enter the main lobby. Bronze statues, paintings, and framed illustrations of boats are seen throughout the building. Over the years, generous members of the Detroit Yacht Club have loaned and donated beautiful art, which is still enjoyed today.

The second-floor lobby ceiling is composed of translucent opaline glass, which gives the effect of daylight illumination. The transition between the wall and the ceiling is decorative plasterwork. Ceramic rondelles are placed above the custom-made sconces, which represent different eras of boating history. In the center, the grand staircase is framed by the wooden balustrade with its turned balusters, finials, and nautical-themed carvings. (ETC.)

The Scripps Trophy from 1911 is on display in the second-floor lobby. It was created by William E. Scripps when he was the commodore of the Detroit Motor Boat Club. The trophy was awarded to the skipper who demonstrated the best navigational skills in a race that lasted several nights. At the base of the trophy, Neptune rides a dolphin and supports a bowl with sea serpent handles. A yacht sits on the top. Scripps was also a Detroit Yacht Club member and gave the trophy to the DYC after the Detroit Motor Boat Club went bankrupt. (DYCC-MS.)

The bronze statue *David* is found on the second floor near the River Vista room. This reproduction of the original by Gianlorenzo Bernini was donated by DYC member Alfred Seymour before he died in 1926. Seymour was well known in Detroit as a boatbuilder and constructed the speedboat *Hornet* for Horace Dodge Sr. (DYCC-MS.)

The bronze statue *St. Joan of Arc* is signed by the artist Adrien-Etienne Gaudez and sits in the main lobby window. Alfred Seymour's daughter Dr. Victory Seymour donated the statue to the Detroit Yacht Club in 1932. During World War I, Dr. Seymour provided moral support to the 32nd Division and the 125th Infantry Regiment, in which her nephew served. After the war, she hosted New Year's Eve parties for the veterans of the regiment, and they made her an honorary member, giving her the title of colonel. (DYCC-MS.)

Commodore Gus Schantz's portrait, painted by Percy Ives in 1925, hangs above the bar in the East Lounge. Ives studied in Paris and at the Pennsylvania Academy of Fine Arts. He also served as dean of the art school of the Detroit Museum of Arts from 1889 to 1892. Ives was an early member of the Scarab Club of Detroit and painted portraits of many prominent Michigan citizens. (DYCC.)

According to the 1955 *Mainsheet*, the Edsel B. Ford Memorial Trophy was awarded to speedboats that raced in the American Power Boat Association's 225-cubic-inch engine class. It is one of several perpetual trophies in the DYC collection. Perpetual trophy winners are awarded the trophy title until a new winner is declared. The Edsel B. Ford Memorial Trophy was rededicated for sailboat racing, and Dave Williams's *Blue Cloud* received the trophy for his first-place finish in the 2009 Off the Dock race series. (DYCC-MS.)

The oil painting *Belle Isle Willows* by Fred Rypsam hangs in the first floor hallway. Rypsam was noted for painting Michigan's snowy winter scenes. He was a life member of the Detroit Yacht Club and the Scarab Club of Detroit. Rypsam built his 40-foot cruiser *Seaway* in his backyard in 1914. He and his wife, Mabel, lived aboard the *Seaway* during the summer months at the Detroit Yacht Club for over 45 years. (DYCC-CN.)

Steady, painted by John George Brown in 1908, hangs on the second floor near the River Vista room. Brown was known for his paintings of children. Dr. Victory Seymour presented the painting to the Detroit Yacht Club in honor of Gen. William Hahn and the men of the 32nd Red Arrow Division who had fought in World War I. The DYC made Dr. Seymour an honorary member of the club in recognition of her generous gifts. (DYCC-CN.)

The Hotel Ste. Claire Cup was first awarded in 1898. William Beyer, general manager of the hotel, provided the trophy. When the 1904 fire destroyed the DYC's Belle Isle clubhouse, it was reported that the Hotel Ste. Claire Cup had been destroyed. However, the previous year's winner actually had the cup in his possession. The cup was an award given at the DYC Sweepstakes Race on Labor Day weekend. It is now in the permanent collection of the DYC Trophy Room. (DYCC-MS.)

This seascape hangs in the Fountain Room. Robert Hopkin was a master marine painter and painted this image of gulls in flight above a stormy sea in 1886. The Detroit Museum of Art showed a retrospective of Hopkin's work in 1907. That year, fellow artists founded a club to support art and artists and called it the Hopkin Club in his honor. Later, it became the Scarab Club of Detroit. Hopkin was born in Scotland in 1832, immigrated with his parents to America in 1843, and died in 1909. (DYCC-CN.)

This mural in the Trophy Room was painted in 1923 by artists W. Francklyn Paris and Frederick J. Wiley of New York. They received the commission after they created a pictorial map for the Children's Room in the main branch of the Detroit Public Library. In the mural, the Detroit Yacht Club is surrounded by canoes, sailboats, speedboats, and a seaplane, suggesting the evolution of water-based transportation. (DYCC-CN.)

The Robert Oakman Trophy is on display in the Trophy Room. At the bottom, the sea rises while sailboats ride the waves. Sea animals surround the helm, which crowns the top. Traditionally, the Robert Oakman Trophy was awarded at an annual dinner and only men were invited. Robert Oakman died in 1942. Four years later, women were invited to attend the Oakman awards for the first time. At that banquet, Oakman's widow, Mamie, presented the trophy to the winner of the catboat race. (DYCC-MS.)

Robert Oakman's yacht *Mamie O* was painted by Percy Ives, well-known portraitist and a founder of the Scarab Club of Detroit. For many years, politicians sought Oakman's advice, which led some to claim that he controlled city hall from the large wicker chair on his luxurious yacht. The painting was presented to the Detroit Yacht Club by his widow, Mamie, and hangs in the club's library. (DYCC-CN.)

Robert Oakman's portrait by Paul Wilhelmi hangs on the wall by the staircase that leads to the third floor. Oakman was the secretary and city assessor for Detroit mayor Hazen Pingree. He followed Pingree to Lansing when Pingree was elected governor, and Oakman was appointed to the Board of State Tax Commissioners. Oakman was a real estate developer and a close friend of the Dodge brothers. As a DYC member, he refused to run for commodore, but at the 1930 annual meeting, the office of honorary commodore was created and bestowed on him. (DYCC-CN.)

Six

YACHT CLUB FUN

The Detroit Yacht Club's organizing principle has always been fun, whether it was renting the steamship *Fortune* for a nighttime cruise in the 1880s or dressing up like pirates in the 1920s. Boating was a shared experience. It might be crewing on a sailboat, cruising in a powerboat, or delighting in the spectacle of boat races. But in fact, more than two thirds of the DYC membership have never been boat owners, and opportunities for other kinds of fun have also drawn people to the club.

When the clubhouse opened in 1923, it had ample room for different activities. The DYC was designed as a family club with a nursery for children and powder rooms, showers, and lockers for women. Men's, women's, and youth swimming drew members. Bowling leagues and bridge games were weekly events. There were junior and adult sailing programs, live sports competitions, speakers, and parties.

As the DYC celebrates its 100th anniversary in its current clubhouse, members still race their sailboats, Venetian Night endures, and the annual Officers' Ball continues. But these days, new social opportunities have replaced old ones. The club now has an outdoor swimming pool with a tiki bar in addition to the indoor pool. The Voyagers, a group that formed in the 1980s, hosts the Christmas Holiday Ball, Meet the Candidates Night, and excursions to local art or theater performances. Volunteers enjoy the camaraderie of decorating every room in the club for Christmas. The Garden Club has published two cookbooks, and members meet for kayaking, bike riding, pickle ball, swimming, and yoga. From pulling weeds with Garden Club friends to dressing up for the Detroit Yacht Club Foundation Gala, there are many possibilities for having fun and making lifelong friends at the club.

Here is the Hotel Ste. Claire, which was located at the northeast corner of Randolph and Monroe Streets. The hotel was a deluxe venue for Detroit's social occasions. The Detroit Yacht Club held its board of director and committee meetings here from 1895 to 1910, and the DYC's first Women's Auxiliary was created at the hotel in 1905. (DHS.)

The Officers' Ball is an annual winter tradition at the Detroit Yacht Club. The Belle Isle clubhouse was usually closed for the winter, so halls and hotels in downtown Detroit hosted the event from 1895 to 1922. Harmonie Hall (pictured), Strasburg's Academy, the Hotel Statler, and the Hotel Pontchartrain were the ballrooms of choice. The current clubhouse has hosted every Officers' Ball since 1923. (BHC.)

Theodore Finney and his orchestra played dance music on the *Frank E. Kirby* steamship and in Detroit ballrooms. Finney mentored many of Detroit's African American musicians, including violinist and bandleader Ben Shook and jazz cornetist W. Jack Johnson, who were important figures in Detroit's ragtime and jazz culture. Finney's Orchestra played for the Detroit Yacht Club Officers' Ball at Harmonie Hall in 1900 and 1901. (BHC.)

The Detroit Yacht Club chartered the steamship *Frank E. Kirby* from 1900 to 1910 for the Put-in-Bay Regatta organized by the Inter-Lake Yachting Association. The steamship was used as a floating grandstand to watch the regatta. After witnessing the sailboat races, passengers stepped ashore for baseball games and picnics. (LC.)

The Hotel Victory was in the Ohio village of Put-in-Bay on South Bass Island in Lake Erie. It had 825 rooms and served as the headquarters for the Inter-Lake Yachting Association's annual regatta. Many Detroit Yacht Club members who came for the regatta stayed here and attended the Yachtsman's Ball in the hotel's magnificent ballroom. (BHC.)

Captain Kidd and his Barnacles worked along piratical lines to boost and promote the Detroit Yacht Club. Barnacle chapters also existed in Chicago, Milwaukee, and New York yacht clubs. Barnacles from several different yacht clubs, including the DYC, staged a mock assault for the grand opening of the Catawba Cliffs Club on Lake Erie in 1929. They entered the club's harbor in full costume and received a simulated "shot and shell" welcome. The DYC Barnacles sold bonds to build the new clubhouse and celebrated its opening with a Pirates' Ball on December 13, 1923. (WSU.)

Flying the skull and crossbones, a boatload of Barnacles prepare to induct new members. This initiation process was capped with a mock execution, walking the plank, and a pledge of loyalty and fidelity to the Detroit Yacht Club. Commodores Gar Wood, Gus Schantz, Alex McLeod, and Harry Kendall were all Barnacles. Visible in the haze at far left is the new DYC clubhouse. (WSU.)

Detroit Yacht Club member Charles Kotcher took his boat the *Betty* M to Miami for the winter. He raced in the Carl Fisher Miami Beach Regatta on Biscayne Bay in February 1916 and won first place in his class. Kotcher owned a home in Miami Beach and invited DYC members to join him for fishing in Florida. He made his fortune in the lumber industry and served as commodore of the Detroit Yacht Club in 1931. (BHC.)

When Detroit Yacht Club members went south for the winter, many stayed at Carl Fisher's Flamingo Hotel in Miami Beach. Fisher owned several hotels and promoted Miami Beach as a winter destination with swimming, tennis, golf, and boxing exhibitions featuring the sports stars of the day. Olympic champ Johnny Weismuller, tennis great Bill Tilden, golfer Gene Sarazen, and boxer Jack Dempsey were hired by Fisher to entertain the tourists. Everyone enjoyed the fact that Prohibition was blatantly ignored in Miami Beach. (HMM.)

The government docks for the US Customs and Border patrol agents were located at Fort Wayne, the historic military post on the Detroit River. During Prohibition, these agents used the Detroit Yacht Club docks as a staging area to catch rumrunners. DYC members who wanted to drink legally crossed the Detroit River into Canadian waters near Peche Island. Their boats joined a raft of a half dozen floating boats known as the Peche Island Yacht Club. According to the *Detroit Free Press*, the DYC was "well known as one of the driest clubs in the city." (WSU.)

Detroit Yacht Club members and guests enjoy a drink on Venetian Night at the DYC bar in 1941. The Twenty-first Amendment to the US Constitution was adopted, and Prohibition was repealed in 1933. Alcohol became legal in America again. The following year, the Detroit Yacht Club received a new lease from the City of Detroit. The lease no longer contained a clause banning the sale of liquor at the club. (LC.)

The American Bowling Congress staged its 1932 national tournament in Detroit. Bowling lanes for the tournament were constructed at the Michigan State Fairgrounds Coliseum in Detroit. Here, Detroit Yacht Club bowlers pose before the beginning of the tournament. In January 1944, more than 100 men representing yacht clubs from Cleveland, Columbus, Toledo, and Sandusky joined bowlers from the Detroit Yacht Club, the Edison Boat Club, and the Grosse Pointe Yacht Club for the annual Inter-Lake Bowling Tournament. (DYCC.)

Detroit Yacht Club bowlers celebrate the 50th anniversary of the DYC's bowling league at their annual awards banquet in 1955. Bowling remained popular, and in 1968, the DYC bowling leagues included multiple groups: the Bowlerettes, East Side Ladies, East Side Men's, Husbands and Wives, Juniors, Ladies, Ladies Day, Mens' Bowling, and Wednesday Niters. (DYCC.)

This advertisement announced a Golden Gloves contest on a Tuesday night at the Detroit Yacht Club. The 1933 *Detroit Free Press* Golden Gloves Tournament featured over 1,400 young men from across the state in a series of boxing bouts in January and February. Two district champions were crowned winners at the DYC on February 7, 1933, and advanced to the semifinals. (DYCC.)

Joe Louis also competed in the 1933 *Detroit Free Press* Golden Gloves Tournament. He was crowned district champion at St. Theresa's Gym on February 13, 1933, and advanced and won the semifinals. At the finals, in front of 13,000 cheering fans, Louis was crowned the Golden Gloves light heavyweight champion at Olympia Stadium on February 22, 1933. He was awarded the *Detroit Free Press* Silver Trophy by the president of the National Boxing Association. (DHS.)

In 1938, the men of the Detroit Yacht Club fielded four baseball teams playing against each other on Belle Isle's baseball diamonds. DYC members, from left to right, Roy Neisch, Don Cunningham, Commodore Al Grundy, Commodore Ray Daley, and Elliott Shumaker played that year. Baseball was a part of the DYC culture. In 1916, the Delray Motor Boat Club, the Edison Boat Club, and the Grosse Pointe Yacht Club joined the DYC and formed the Warm Mitt Society and played baseball at Put-in-Bay regattas. (DYCC-CN.)

The seventh annual Detroit Yacht Club All American Sports Banquet on January 25, 1941, included live boxing, wrestling, and fencing and a star-studded guest list. Among the guests was Bobo Newsom, who pitched 21 wins out of 26 starts and led the Detroit Tigers to the American League pennant in 1940. Other guests included George Halas, owner and coach of the Chicago Bears, winners of the 1940 NFL championship game, and Clark Shaughnessy, coach of Stanford's football team that won the 1941 Rose Bowl. (EHSC.)

An event combining fun and tradition at the Detroit Yacht Club is the annual Officers' Ball. The evening begins with herald trumpets signaling the arrival of many guests, including visiting commodores, dignitaries, DYC commodores, directors, fleet officers, and trustees. A glass is raised to the queen of England and to the office of the president of the United States and is followed by more toasting, dinner, and then the grand march and dancing in the ballroom. (DYCC.)

Commodore Joe Brooks and his wife, Lady Dara Brooks, lead the grand march into the DYC ballroom in January 2015. At the start of the grand march, floor managers help form the couples into a line to enter the ballroom. After the commodore and his wife lead a general promenade around the room, the floor managers pair the couples into quartets and octets to conclude the marching. Then the colors are presented, the national anthems of Canada and the United States are played, and an evening of dancing commences. (DYCC.)

Square dancing was a regular occurrence in the DYC ballroom in the 1920s, 1930s, and 1940s. The caller at the microphone leads the dance steps for those on the floor. Detroit Yacht Club member Henry Ford promoted "olde tyme" dancing. Benjamin Lovett was a full-time dance instructor hired by Ford to teach schottisches, reels, and polkas to Ford employees, students, and the general public. Lovett attended DYC dances and occasionally taught at the club. (DYCC.)

At the 2001 Officers' Ball, Commodore Dorothy O'Brien invited Shirley Glass to be her guest. Glass was the first woman to serve on the DYC board of directors in 1982. Dorothy O'Brien, a powerboater, served in 2001 as the first female commodore of the club. (DHS.)

The Detroit Yacht Club sponsored its first iceboat race in 1895. Iceboating on Lake St. Clair was not for the faint of heart. It required sailing ability and nerve as the boats traveled at high speeds on the ice. Here, Mrs. Gus Miller races her iceboat during the winter of 1946 and received a first-place flag. She celebrated her victory at the Detroit Yacht Club iceboat awards ceremony on March 3, 1946. (DYCC.)

In the 1960s and 1970s, the Pelicans met every Friday for lunch at the Detroit Yacht Club. Professional, political, and business leaders were invited to speak. Average attendance was approximately 100 men. When Jimmy Hoffa, president of the Teamsters Union, was the Pelicans' guest speaker on April 19, 1963, over 640 men were present. It was the largest crowd ever to attend a Pelicans' luncheon. In recent years, the Pelicans meet monthly to hear a variety of speakers. (WSU.)

An annual tradition of the Detroit Yacht Club is the Father's Day Antique and Classic Boat Review. DYC members bring their historic cars and boats to the club for all to admire. This rare 1936 Cadillac Series 60 V-8 business coupe with optional dual side-mounted spare tires was a hit at the 2004 show. (DYCC.)

In 1941, the Detroit Yacht Club Sea Gulls were swimming every Tuesday. The Sea Gulls competed for the annual Paddle Trophy against other clubs, a swimming marathon over three days typically with no limit to the hours of swimming allowed. The December 1941 contest was won by the YWCA downtown branch with 56 miles. The DYC finished second with 51.5 miles. (DYCC.)

The National Amateur Athletic Union (AAU) Senior Women's Outdoor Swimming and Diving Championships were held on Belle Isle in 1925. The Detroit Yacht Club hosted the event and built this 30-foot diving tower for the competition. The tower was located where Midway Dock's well No. 32 is today. The AAU was founded in 1888 and served as the national governing body for amateur sports for many years. (WSU.)

Crowds watch the AAU National Platform Diving Championships on August 27, 1927. The DYC continued to host swimming championship events, including the state diving championships in 1926, state swimming and diving championships in 1933, and National Junior AAU Platform Diving Championships in 1937. The DYC swimming program continues to be an important part of the club's activities for children and young adults. (WSU.)

All-Star Swimming Meet

Los Angeles A. C. and Allied Clubs

vs.

Combined D. Y. C., D. A. C. and
U. of M. Teams

Thursday Evening, April 7th

8:15 P. M.

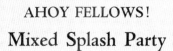

AHOY FELLOWS!

Mixed Splash Party

Monday Evening, April 18th

Single men may bring their girls to this party. There will be eats, entertainment and fun for all. Under the auspices of the Sea Gull Class.

Both meets in D. Y. C. Pool.

The Detroit Yacht Club hosted an All-Star Swimming Meet in 1932. The Los Angeles Athletic Club brought star swimmers Buster Crabbe, Mickey Riley, and Dutch Smith. They competed against a combined team from the DYC, the Detroit Athletic Club, and the University of Michigan. The Los Angeles team won seven of the eight races. Almost 600 spectators jammed into the DYC natatorium to watch the competition. Crabbe, Riley, and Smith went on to win gold medals four months later at the 1932 Olympics in Los Angeles. (DYCC.)

Jane Cadwell was a star on the Detroit Yacht Club and Northwestern High School swim teams. She qualified for the Women's National Senior Swimming Championship in Los Angeles, but as an honor student, did not want to miss school to swim in the meet. Her high school principal and her father urged her to accept the invitation, and her father promised she could fly to the meet. Cadwell won the 100-yard breaststroke race on April 29, 1932. Four months later, she returned to Los Angeles and swam the 200-meter breaststroke in the Olympics and finished seventh. (WSU.)

Ten days after the Detroit Yacht Club held a grand opening for its new clubhouse, 132 swimmers competed in the first swim meet held in the club's indoor pool on June 9, 1923. Water sports have always been popular at the club. The Sea Serpents (pictured) are one of the oldest clubs in the DYC. Here, they are taking practice shots and getting ready for a water basketball game in the clubhouse natatorium. (DYCC-CN.)

The Sea Gulls' Tuesday schedule included a morning swim in the pool followed by lunch. After their luncheon, the Sea Gulls filled Peacock Alley with 15 tables of bridge. Men and women played bridge every second and fourth Tuesday. As more women started working outside of the home, the Sea Gulls stopped their morning swim. Today, the Sea Gulls are a dynamic, fun-loving group who are there to help others. They still play bridge once a week. (DYCC.)

The 1999 Memorial Day swim meet at the Detroit Yacht Club outdoor pool splashed off with a floating American flag. The new outdoor pool replaced a 1962 pool that could no longer be used for swim meets because it was too shallow to safely use starting blocks. Two layers of reinforcing steel and concrete floors seven feet thick were used in its construction. Two Olympic gold medalists dedicated the pool by dipping their medals into the water in 1998. (MAC.)

The Detroit Yacht Club swim team competes in a 2010 Michigan Inter-club Swimming Association (MICSA) swim meet. The International Swimming Hall of Fame credited MICSA as being the first organized swimming league of private clubs that held league championships based on age groups. The DYC was a founding member, and there are now 14 member clubs. (DYCC.)

The docks and boats at the Detroit Yacht Club sparkle with lights, and fireworks set the harbor aglow for the club's annual splash of merriment called Venetian Night. Strolling troubadours serenade people on the docks, and dancing under the stars concludes the evening. This outdoor carnival preceded the Sweepstakes and Harmsworth Trophy races in September 1931. (WSU.)

Commodore Elliott Shumaker and his wife, Jane, aboard their anchored flagship, exchange salutes as the fleet of the Detroit Yacht Club parades past them on August 26, 1941. The fleet review was the opening ceremony for Venetian Night. It was followed by cocktail parties aboard yachts, dinner in the clubhouse, and music and dancing. (LC.)

Detroit Yacht Club general manager Robert Thompson watches his chefs prepare the Venetian Night dinner on August 26, 1941. Thompson began as a bellboy at the Hotel Statler in Detroit in 1919 and advanced to become the hotel's assistant manager. In 1935, he joined the DYC as the general manager, supervising a staff of 112. (LC.)

Waitstaff in starched uniforms serve dinner on Venetian Night in the Fountain Room on August 26, 1941. The DYC had recently installed two presses in the laundry room due to the hundreds of uniforms required every week for the dock crew, waiters, waitresses, bartenders, and maids. (LC.)

In the 1930s, the club created temporary outdoor dance floors for the summer months. Dancing was so popular that Starlight Circle was constructed in 1941, and became the club's permanent outdoor dance floor. It was a hit for the 1941 Venetian Night dance shown here. In 1948, the dance floor was just as crowded for Tommy Dorsey and his Orchestra on Venetian Night. (LC.)

A horse is hitched to the railing at the entrance to the Dead End Dude Ranch at the Detroit Yacht Club. Dead End Dock was decorated in a Western theme for Venetian Night in the 1970s. Michigan yacht clubs started celebrating Venetian Night in 1901 when the Macatawa Bay Yacht Club, just west of Holland, Michigan, held its first Venetian Night with a regatta followed by an evening of dining, dancing, and illuminated boats. (BFC.)

Commodore Lucius Tripp, MD, and his wife, Delores, enjoy the start of the 2002 Venetian Night festivities. Dr. Tripp, a neurosurgeon, applied to join the club in the 1970s but was denied. He was an avid boater and wanted to join the club. As he explained in a 2002 interview with the *Detroit Free Press*, he knew one day the DYC would accept him. He and Delores joined the club in the 1980s. Their boat, *Dr. T.*, was a Tiara 43 convertible powerboat. In 2002, Dr. Tripp became the first African American to serve as commodore of the Detroit Yacht Club. (DYCC.)

The DYC Kayak Club paddles past the Detroit Renaissance Center. Kayakers at the Detroit Yacht Club are led by Lisa Bartnik and Hugh Cairns, who organize paddles through the Blue Heron Lagoon and Lake Okonoka on Belle Isle, sunrise and sunset paddles, and a trip through the Detroit River canals. For those ready for a bigger challenge, the Kayak Club also holds a Once Around Belle Isle paddle. (DYCC.)

The city of Chatham, Ontario, first invited the Detroit Yacht Club to visit in 1927. The DYC boaters were met at the mouth of the Thames River by a reception committee and escorted upstream to town. Guest privileges for the weekend included lunch in the armory, golfing at the Chatham Golf and Country Club, and a Yachtsmen's Ball in the evening. Here, DYC powerboats are anchored in the Thames after a 1972 cruise to Chatham. (BFC.)

The Detroit Yacht Club has an annual Fleet Rendezvous in the fall. In the 1930s, the rendezvous included a corn roast, fat sailor's race, ladies' nail driving contest, baseball game, and a tug-of-war pitting married men against single men. Now the weekend includes a chili cook-off, doggie parade, pumpkin carving, trick or treating, football, and live music. Commodore A.J. Telmos, MD, and his wife, Candis, attended the 2015 DYC Frostbite Rendezvous at Lake St. Clair Metropark. (DYCC.)

Commodore Fred Carr, co-chair of the Detroit Yacht Club Rod and Gun Club, poses by the Browns Bay Inn bragging stick at Wolfe Island in Canada. The Rod and Gun Club hosts an annual walleye tournament, a fun family fishing day, and a wild game dinner. The club occasionally organizes special trips and recently traveled to Argentina for big game hunting. (DYCC.)

Sandra and David Smith are all smiles in 2014 at the annual Candidates Wine Tasting in the Grill Restaurant. The Voyageurs sponsor the event on the Friday before the election of club officers. Candidates introduce themselves as they pour the wine. Members have the opportunity to taste a wide variety of wines, enjoy a strolling dinner among friends, and get to know who is running for election. (DYCC.)

The Sistine Chapel Choir came to the United States in 2017 for the first time in 30 years. The choir, which sings for the pope's Masses, performed in concert at the Detroit Opera House. Commodore Patricia Thull O'Brien, the second woman elected commodore of the Detroit Yacht Club, and Msgr. Charles Kosanke, DYC fleet chaplain, arranged for the choir to enjoy lunch at the club when they visited Detroit. The choir poses on the broad outdoor staircase between Commodore O'Brien and Monsignor Kosanke. (PTOC.)

Seven

RESTORING
THE GRANDEUR

Gus Schantz, Gar Wood, and the board of directors had the imagination and courage in the early 1920s to build a clubhouse unrivaled in size or grandeur. No yacht club on this scale had ever existed on the Great Lakes. A project this size required active and devoted members. They met the challenge.

Succeeding generations stepped forward to maintain the building. Traditions changed, and rooms were reimagined. The gymnasium became a lounge, the carpenter shop became the bar, and the boatmen's room became the Port Haven Lounge. Penny Breck sanded and refinished the paneling in the ballroom and the East Lounge. The Sea Gulls and the Voyageurs donated money for the restoration of the fountain in the main dining room.

As the building aged, restoration needs increased. Structural, plumbing, and roof repairs were essential to the building's survival. The clubhouse was listed in the National Register of Historic Places in 2011, and the Detroit Yacht Club Foundation was approved as a 501(c)3 nonprofit the next year. The foundation became the locus for revitalization of the clubhouse. For example, windows were replaced, the roof was fixed, and an accessible entrance was created. More than 30 restoration projects have been completed with the support of voluntary donations from members and DYC Foundation fundraising events.

Repairing and maintaining such a treasure takes time and care. Today, the foundation, with the active support of the board of directors, has laid the groundwork for the natatorium's much-needed renovation. A highly experienced restoration and construction professional has been hired to guide the project and recommend the contractors. Fundraising for the natatorium is led by Mark Lifter and Robin Heller of the Detroit Yacht Club Foundation. The foundation's annual gala is a fabulous event not to be missed and continues the tradition of devoted members paying forward the debt to past generations. Restoring the grandeur continues.

In 1952, this fountain was partially demolished and sealed up to provide more space in the dining room. Rumors of a fountain hidden behind the walls of the main dining room led to its rediscovery in 1993. Member donations funded the reconstruction and restoration of the fountain. The clubhouse was completed in 1923 with two fountains. Mary Chase Stratton's Pewabic Pottery billed the architect George Mason for the sunporch fountain, and the fountain pictured here was built at the same time. Perhaps Pewabic Pottery built both, but no documentation has been found to confirm its provenance. (DYCC-CN.)

On the east side of the clubhouse, a rooftop projector room was added in 1953 to show 35-mm movies in the ballroom. Phase one of the Detroit Yacht Club Foundation work included the demolition of the problematic projector room and repair of roof leaks. Masonry, glass block, a structural support beam, and damaged tile were replaced. Phase one was started in 2014 and finished as part of phase two in September 2016. (DYCF.)

Addressing persistent leaks required more than removing the projector room. Engineering and contractor analysis identified six areas of the roof in need of comprehensive repair. In 2019, the weather cooperated, and the work was completed during the winter. (DYCF.)

The main entrance consisted of wooden revolving doors set in a stonework frame over which King Neptune keeps watch. To preserve this historic archway and enhance accessibility to the clubhouse, the DYC built a new doorway. The temporary white door to the left of the main entrance was later upgraded to provide an accessible entrance. A ribbon-cutting ceremony officially opened the new entrance on the night of the 2017 annual Officers' Ball. (DYCF.)

Lamar Hankins repairs the plaster walls and ceiling damaged by the leaking roof in the East Lounge. The restoration work occurred while the clubhouse was closed in 2020 due to the pandemic. (DYCF.)

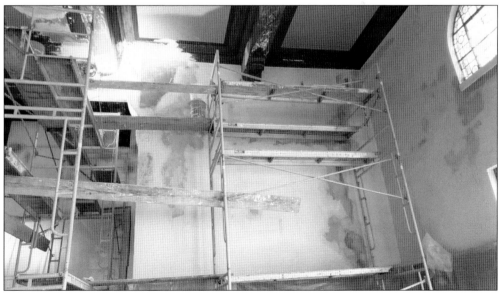

After the plaster was repaired in the East Lounge, it was time to start work restoring the decorative stenciling on the beams. These beams are concrete and completely fireproof. After the specialists from Paintwork Detroit finished their work, the beams appeared like wood. (DYCF.)

The walls and ceiling plaster of the sunporch, which is adjacent to the East Lounge, were repaired in July 2020. Molds were made to recreate the plaster roping and relief that was damaged or missing. (DYCF.)

The restoration of the sunporch was finished in April 2021. The sea serpent fountain at the far end of the room sprays water from its mouth into a bowl, which then flows into a lower bowl. Pewabic Pottery installed this fountain on May 25, 1923. William Stratton, the husband of Mary Chase Stratton of Pewabic Pottery, was a close associate and former employee of Mason. (DYCC-CN.)

Detroit Yacht Club general manager Rick Price admires the new finish that Michigan Hardwood Floors employee Mark Rowe is applying to the freshly sanded ballroom floor. The DYC Preservation Fund paid to replace the wood that was damaged and had the entire floor sanded and refinished. (DYCC.)

The stenciling on the beams is finished, and the ship above the fireplace has been restored in this 2021 photograph. The Detroit Yacht Club Foundation raises money through a variety of activities, including the sponsorship of big band dances. Dancing at the Grand began in 2014 and is held three times a year. These dances have raised over $50,000 for the foundation. The grandeur is returning because the membership, board of directors, foundation, and the preservation fund have embraced the challenge of maintaining a fabulous clubhouse for future generations. (DYCC-CN.)

DISCOVER THOUSANDS OF LOCAL HISTORY BOOKS FEATURING MILLIONS OF VINTAGE IMAGES

Arcadia Publishing, the leading local history publisher in the United States, is committed to making history accessible and meaningful through publishing books that celebrate and preserve the heritage of America's people and places.

Find more books like this at
www.arcadiapublishing.com

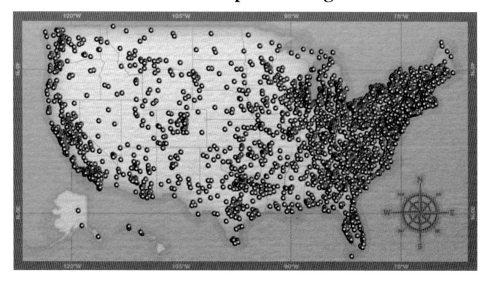

Search for your hometown history, your old stomping grounds, and even your favorite sports team.

Consistent with our mission to preserve history on a local level, this book was printed in South Carolina on American-made paper and manufactured entirely in the United States. Products carrying the accredited Forest Stewardship Council (FSC) label are printed on 100 percent FSC-certified paper.

MADE IN THE USA